Denis Hermann

Kirmānī Shaykhism and the *ijtihād*

BIBLIOTHECA ACADEMICA

Reihe

Orientalistik

Band 24

ERGON VERLAG

Denis Hermann

Kirmānī Shaykhism and the *ijtihād*

A Study of Abū al-Qāsim Khān Ibrāhīmī's *Ijtihād wa taqlīd*

ERGON VERLAG

Bibliografische Information der Deutschen Nationalbibliothek
Die Deutsche Nationalbibliothek verzeichnet diese Publikation in der Deutschen Nationalbibliografie; detaillierte bibliografische Daten sind im Internet über http://dnb.d-nb.de abrufbar.

Bibliographic information published by the Deutsche Nationalbibliothek
The Deutsche Nationalbibliothek lists this publication in the Deutsche Nationalbibliografie; detailed bibliographic data are available in the Internet at http://dnb.dnb.de.

Gedruckt auf alterungsbeständigem Papier.
Satz: Thomas Breier, Ergon-Verlag GmbH
Umschlaggestaltung: Jan von Hugo

www.ergon-verlag.de

ISBN 978-3-95650-097-8
ISSN 1866-5071

Contents

Introduction

This research is a study of Abū al-Qāsim Khān Ibrāhīmī [Abū al-Qāsim Khān] (d. 1969)'s *Ijtihād wa taqlīd*, a contemporary Shaykhī Kirmānī literary text. This work is a particularly clear exposé of Shaykhī Kirmānī opinions on *ijtihad*, on the structure and hierarchy of the Shi'i community as proposed by the *uṣūlī* clergy, and, more broadly, on the intellectual history of Usulism. Starting in the mid-seventeenth century, the *akhbārī* movement and, in particular, Muḥammad Amīn al-Astarābādī (d. 1036/1627) had already challenged Usulism and the reliance on *ijtihād*; al-Astarābādī summarized his thinking in his *al-Fawā'id al-madaniyya* [Informative Points from Medina]. In particular, he refused to consider *'aql* (reason) and *ijmā'* (consensus) as "legal principles" (*uṣūl-i fiqh*) and only, therefore, recognized the Qur'ān and the *ḥadīth*. He also proposed a revision of the history of Shi'ism, with the great legal scholar al-'Allāma al-Ḥillī (d. 726/1325), whom he reproached for several innovations, as his primary target. These innovations included the development of models for classifying *ḥadīth*s according to the Sunni model; the development of the doctrine of *ijtihād*, inspired by analogical reasoning (*qiyās*); and the resulting division of the Shi'i community into two groups, with the *mujtahid*s on one side and the *muqallid*s on the other. According to *uṣūlī* doctrine, the *muqallid*s are imitators, compelled to observe their *taqlīd* (imitation) following a living *mujtahid* who is, therefore, capable of carrying out *ijtihād*, the independent effort to interpret the law. Muḥammad Amīn al-Astarābādī saw these doctrinal developments as being influenced by Sunnism and, in particular, by Shafi'ism, the legal tradition (*madhhab*) in which many of the great Shi'i legal scholars (*fuqahā*)–such as al-'Allāma al-Ḥillī, al-Shahīd al-Awwal (d. 786/1384), 'Alī b. 'Abd al-'Ālī al-Karakī (d. 940/1534), al-Shahīd al-Thānī (d. 965/1558), Ḥusayn b. 'Abd al-Ṣamad al-'Āmilī (d. 984/1576), and Bahā al-Dīn al-'Āmilī (d. 1030/1621)–received their training.[1]

The period following the Major Occultation (*ghaybat-i kubrā*) of the twelfth Shi'i Imām in 329/940-941 plunged his followers into a period known as the period of "doubt" or of "perplexity" (*ḥayra*). The main currents of Imami Shi'ism–Sufism, Usulism, Akhbarism, and, later, Shaykhism–developed around the response to this problematic and painful absence of the Imām, the supreme authority. The positions held by these various currents towards the *fiqh* shed light on the meaning that they assign to the Occultation and to the way in which Shi'as must understand this absence. And although we have known the positions of *akhbārī* and *uṣūlī* ulemas on *ijtihād* for several decades, that of the Sufi Shi'as was poorly

1 See the more extended list proposed by Devin J. Stewart in *Islamic Legal Orthodoxy. Twelver Shiite Reponses to the Sunni Legal System*, Salt Lake City: The University of Utah Press, 1998, pp. 65-95. On the reasons that drove many Shi'i legal scholars to form themselves into Shafi'ite madrasas rather than Hanafite, Hanbalite, or Malikite ones, see ibid., pp. 102-106.

documented until very recently. Now, however, we know that although the Sufi Shiʿi masters of the Qajar period and the present did not write many *fiqh* treatises nor make a point of their own status as legal scholars (*fuqahā*) with respect to their disciples (*murīd*), it is nevertheless the case that many of them were trained by the greatest *mujtahid*s of their times, that they recognized the "legal principles" (*uṣūl-i fiqh*) of Usulism, and that they often attained the rank of *mujtahid* without, however, necessarily practicing *ijtihād* nor creating a relationship with their disciples like that between a *mujtahid* and a *muqallid*.[2]

The writings by Shaykhī Kirmānī masters on law (*fiqh*), in particular, have been largely ignored because it is the theosophical analysis of the founder of the school, Shaykh Aḥmad al-Aḥsā'ī's (d. 1241/1826), that has gained the attention of researchers interested in Shaykhism.[3] And yet the Shaykhī Kirmānī masters who came before Abū al-Qāsim Khān wrote more than a hundred and seventy treatises dealing specifically with *fiqh*.[4] And even though the Shaykhī Kirmānī' epistemological stance of rejecting *ijtihād* and *'aql* as a "legal principle" (*uṣūl-i fiqh*) had already been developed before the publication of *Ijtihād wa taqlīd*, it was nevertheless necessary, in order to begin this line of argumentation, to first examine the

2 See Shahram Pazouki, "*Fiqh* et soufisme à la période qajare: quelques notes sur l'œuvre juridique des maîtres niʿmatullāhī gunābādī," in Denis Hermann and Sabrina Mervin (ed.), *Shiʿi Trends and Dynamics in Modern Times (XVIIIth-XXth centuries). Courants et dynamiques chiites à l'époque moderne (XVIIIe-XXe siècles)*, Beirut : OIB-IFRI, 2010, pp. 113-127.

3 See Juan Cole, "Casting Away the Self: The Mysticism of Shaikh Ahmad al-Ahsâ'î," in Rainer Brunner and Werner Ende (ed.), *The Twelver Shia in Modern Times. Religious Culture & Political History*, Leiden: Brill, 2001, pp. 25-37; idem, "Individualism and the Spiritual Path in Shaikh Ahmad al-Ahsa'i," in L. Clarke (ed.), *Shi'ite Heritage: Essays on Classical and Modern Traditions*, New York : Binghamton, 2001, pp. 345-358; idem, "Shaikh Ahmad al-Ahsa'i on the Sources of Religious Authority," in Linda Walbridge (ed.), *The Most Learned of the Shi'a: The Institution of the Marja' Taqlid*, Oxford: Oxford University Press, 2001, pp. 82-93; idem, "The World as Text: Cosmologies of Shaikh Ahmad al-Ahsaʿi," *Studia Islamica*, vol. 80 (1994), pp. 145-163; Todd Lawson, "Orthodoxy and Heterodoxy in Twelver Shiʿism: Aḥmad al-Aḥsā'ī on Fayḍ Kāshānī (the *Risālat al-'Ilmiyya*)," in Robert Gleave (ed.), *Religion and Society in Qajar Iran*, London-New York: Routledge Curzon, 2005, pp. 127-154; idem, "Shaikh Aḥmad al-Aḥsā'ī and the World of Images," in *Shiʿi Trends and Dynamics in Modern Times (XVIIIth-XXth centuries)*, pp. 19-31; idem, "The Hidden Words of Fayḍ Kāshāni," in Maria Szuppe (ed.), *Iran. Questions et connaissances. Actes du IVe congrès européen des études iraniennes, organisé par la Societas Iranologica Europaea, Paris, 6-10 septembre 1999*, vol. II : *Périodes médiévale et moderne*, Paris : Studia Iranica, Cahier 26, 2002, pp. 427-447; Idris S. Hamid, "The Metaphysics and Cosmology of Process According to Shaikh Aḥmad al-Aḥsā'ī: Critical Edition, Translation and Analysis of 'Observations in Wisdom'" (Ph.D. dissertation, State University of New York, 1998); Vahid Rafati, "The Development of Shaikhī Thought in Shīʿī Islam" (Ph.D. dissertation, UCLA, 1979), pp. 85-89; Denis M. MacEoin, "From Shaikhism to Babism, a Study in Charismatic Renewal in Shîʿî Islam," in Denis M. MacEoin, *The Messiah of Shiraz. Studies in Early and Middle Babism*, Leiden: Brill, 2009, pp. 3-249; idem, "Cosmogony and Cosmology. vii. In Shaikhism," *Encyclopaedia Iranica*, vol. VI, 1993, pp. 326-328.

4 These can be found listed in the catalogue of the works of the masters of the school compiled by Abū al-Qāsim Khān Ibrāhīmī himself, *Fihrist-i kutub-i mashāyikh-i 'iẓām*, Kerman: Saʿādat, 3rd ed., 1977, pp. 309-314, 390-403, 481-497, 620-626, and 699-705.

much more technical writings. In addition, it should be said that the Shaykhī Kirmānī literature on *ijtihād* did not put as much emphasis on the intellectual history of *ijtihād* in the Imami Shi'i milieu.

Ijtihād wa taqlīd, then, revived and updated a very old controversy pitting the traditionalist *akhbārīs* against the rationalist *uṣūlīs*, adding new elements to the debate. We can already point out some of the elements that are specific and original to this work. First, Abū al-Qāsim Khān proposes a return to the original meaning of the concept of *ijtihād*, namely effort, in this case the effort to understand the teaching of the Imams. With respect to this concept he introduces a fundamental distinction, if not an outright contradiction, to the meaning given to it by the *uṣūlī mujtahids*. Abū al-Qāsim Khān professes himself to be saddened by the evolution of Shi'ism, a religion that is monopolized by a clergy that is for the most part more interested in increasing its own authority and power over the masses than in introducing those masses to the teaching of the Imams. Faced with this unnatural orientation of Shi'ism, he wishes to speak to the entire community of Shi'as at a time of great political confusion in Iran, given that this work was written in 1943, not long after Riḍā Shāh's abdication in September of 1941 and his subsequent exile to South Africa. Those years may well have been a good time to write such a treatise, since the *uṣūlī* religious schools (*ḥawza-yi 'ilmiyya*) were in a very precarious position and their ability to respond to minorities within Shi'ism was more limited than usual.[5] Abū al-Qāsim Khān composed a particularly comprehensible work, accessible to everyone, with which he desired to contribute to a greater understanding of *fiqh* and of *ijtihād* in that pivotal period. The years 1930 to 1950 were marked by considerable societal changes, including a measurable increase in the literacy rate; it is, therefore, highly likely that laypeople were reading more religious literature than they had in earlier times. For this reason, the format and style of *Ijtihād wa taqlīd* were particularly well-suited to these new conditions. From then on, this treatise could be read and understand by every Shi'a, even without legal training, unlike the *akhbārī* legal treatises that were written during the Safavid period (906-1134/1501-1722), such as *al-Fawā'id al-madaniyya*. It could be tempting to compare the positions taken in *Ijtihād wa taqlīd* with those of the *akhbārī* scholars, but Abū al-Qāsim Khān suggests that the argumentation of those scholars should be "overtaken" by using the doctrine of the *rukn-i rābi'* (the fourth pillar) on the occult and non-occult hierarchization of Shi'as. Therefore, it emphasizes, probably more than is done in Akhbarism, the central position held by the elite ulemas in the teaching of *fiqh*.

After introducing Shaykhism and, in particular, the doctrine of the *rukn-i rābi'*, which is essential for understanding the originality of Abū al-Qāsim Khān's argumentation on the subject of *ijtihād*, and after we have looked at the life and work

---

5 See Shahrough Akhavi in *Religion and Politics in Contemporary Iran. Clergy-State Relations in the Pahlavi Period*, Albany, New York: State University of New York Press, 1980, pp. 60-61.

of this author as well as the main historical connections between Shaykhism and Akhbarism, we will examine the main themes of *Ijtihād wa taqlīd*, paying particular attention to the introduction to the concepts of *ijtihād* and *muqallid*, the origins of *ijtihād* within Shi'ism, the connections between reason (*'aql*) and *fiqh*, and, finally, Abū al-Qāsim Khān's own proposals.

Although I do not believe that it is in any way necessary to be a specialist in Shi'i *fiqh* in order to study the line of argumentation developed by Abū al-Qāsim Khān in his *Ijtihād wa taqlīd*, I do want to emphasize the point that such a study is of course nothing more than an introduction to Islamic legal scholarship and to *ijtihād* as understood by Kirmānī Shaykhism. A more thorough analysis by scholars of Muslim and Shi'i law of the treatises on *fiqh* by Shaykhī Kirmānī masters that preceded *Ijtihād wa taqlīd* is still necessary and would constitute a notable advance in our knowledge of the intellectual and doctrinal history of Twelver Shi'ism.

I. The Rise of Shaykhism

Shaykhism arose in the late eighteenth century, in the *'atabāt* (Shiʿi shrine cities in Iraq), from the teachings of Shaykh Aḥmad al-Aḥsā'ī (d. 1241/1826), a religious scholar from Al-Aḥsā, in the eastern part of the Arabian Peninsula. The shaykh mostly studied and taught in the *'atabāt* cities of Iraq until 1806; after that, he lived almost entirely in Iran, chiefly in Yazd and Kermānshāh. In 1824, two years before his death, he was the object of a *takfīr* (excommunication) by a rationalist cleric from Qazwīn, Mūllā Muḥammad-Taqī Baraghānī (d. 1263/1847).[1] The cleric accused the shaykh of denying the return of the physical body at the moment of *ma'ād* (resurrection), which is considered a dogma in Islam. Shaykh Aḥmad al-Aḥsā'ī's position on philosophy, on speculative mysticism, and in particular on the question of *ma'ād*, is extremely complex, and it is likely that Mūllā Muḥammad-Taqī Baraghānī did not understand the shaykh's explanations of his position. The Shaykhī school can be said to have been born after the shaykh's excommunication and death; it was organized and structured under the direction of one of his most devoted pupils, Sayyid Kāẓim Rashtī (d. 1259/1843), who taught mostly in Karbala, which was at that time home to the most important Shiʿi scholars. So now, not that long after the decline and quasi-extinction of the Akhbārī school following the murder of Muḥammad Akhbārī Nayshābūrī (d. 1233/1818),[2] Twelver Shi'ism was again marked by a new fracture. While the majority agreed with the rationalist *uṣūlī* school, a minority rallied to the new school that was being established under the leadership of Sayyid Kāẓim Rashtī.[3] When he died in 1843, several of his pupils vied (as is often the case when an important spiritual leader dies) for the leadership of the young Shaykhī school. Muḥammad Karīm Khān Kirmānī [Muḥammad Karīm Khān] (d. 1288/1871), who was an ancestor of the author of *Ijtihād wa taqlīd*, founded the so-called "Kirmānī" branch. His father, Muḥammad Ibrāhīm Khān Zahīr al-Dawla (d. 1240/1824), had been a member of the Qajar family and governor of Kerman and of the Baluchistan province. Mullā Mu-

1 For more information on Mūllā Muḥammad-Taqī Baraghānī, see MacEoin, "Baraghānī, Mollā Moḥammad-Taqī," *Encyclopaedia Iranica*, vol. III, 1989, p. 740; and Moojan Momen, "Usuli, Akhbari, Shaikhi, Babi: The Tribulations of a Qazvin Family," *Iranian Studies*, vol. 36/3 (2003), pp. 317-337, especially pp. 320, 321, 323, and 324.

2 On the decline of Akhbarism after Muḥammad Akhbārī Nayshābūrī's assassination, see Gleave, *Scripturalist Islam. The History and Doctrines of the Akhbārī Shīʿī School*, Leiden: Brill, 2007.

3 On the development of Shaykhism in Karbala under the leadership of Sayyid Kāẓim Rashtī, see Cole and Momen, "Mafia, Mob and Shi'ism in Iraq: The Rebellion of Ottoman Kerbala, 1824-1843," *Past and Present*, vol. 112 (1986), pp. 112-143; Cole, "'Indian Money' and the Shi'i Shrine cities of Iraq 1786-1850," *Middle Eastern Studies*, vol. 22/4 (1986), pp. 461-480; Momen, "Usuli"; Meir Litvak, *Shi'i Scholars of Nineteenth-Century Iraq. The 'ulama' of Najaf and Karbala'*, Cambridge: Cambridge University Press, 1998; and Litvak, "Failed Manipulation: The British, the Oudh Bequest and the Shi'i Ulama' of Najaf and Karbala," *British Journal of Middle Eastern Studies*, vol. 27/1 (2000), pp. 68-89.

ḥammad Māmaqānī (d. 1269/1852), Ḥājj Mīrzā Shafī' Thiqat al-Islām-i Tabrīzī (d. 1301/1884) and Mīrzā Muḥammad Bāqir Uskū'ī (d. 1301/1883), meanwhile, founded the so-called "Tabrīzī" or "Tabrīzī-Karbalā'ī" branch.[4] There are two principal doctrinal differences between these two branches: the Shaykhī Tabrīzīs do not reject the use of *ijtihād* and do not acknowledge the "fourth pillar" (*rukn-i rābi'*). The Tabrīzī masters were as such less interested in *ḥadīth* and stressed the legitimacy of *ijtihād* very clearly in their treatises, even if its use appears to be more constrained and limited than in Usulism.

The Shaykhī Kirmānī school, which does not acknowledge the religious legitimacy of the legal scholars and especially not of the *mujtahid*s, is, at the same time, based on a traditional and charismatic authority. On the one hand, Kirmānī Shaykhism affirms a return to the fundamentals of Shi'i Islam, that is to say the teachings of the Prophet and the Imams as expressed in the *ḥadīth*. On the other hand, it points out the fact that the teachings of Shaykh Aḥmad al-Aḥsā'ī and Sayyid Kāẓim Rashtī were directly inspired by the Prophet and the Imams and, in particular, the Hidden Imām. This explains why, at the beginning of the nineteenth century, the Shaykhīs called themselves *kashfiyya* (disclosers). In terms of their approach to the law, then, and also given the great importance they place on the study of the *ḥadīth*, the Shaykhī Kirmānīs would seem to be a continuation of Akhbarism. In addition, this Shaykhī Kirmānī position on the prohibition on using *ijtihād* as the basis for legal rulings (*ḥukm*) also has obvious implications for their views on politics. Thus, many of the Shaykhī writings, while not touching directly on the question of the relationship between religion and politics, nevertheless come back, by association, to the claims of certain ulemas to political power.[5] The breadth and the diversity of the religious literature composed by the various scholars within Shaykhism starting in the early nineteenth century clearly makes this school one of the most prolific movements within the modern and contemporary intellectual history of Shi'ism.

The "Fourth Pillar" (rukn-i rābi')

Now let us summarize the doctrine of the *rukn-i rābi'*, as developed mainly by Muḥammad Karīm Khān, in order to understand the rhetoric of Kirmānī Shaykhism and of Abū al-Qāsim Khān regarding *fiqh*. From the eighteenth century on-

---

4 On the Tabrīzī branch, see Hermann, *Le shaykhisme à la période qajare. Histoire sociale et doctrinale d'une École chiite*, Turnhoult: Brepols, forthcoming; Christoph Werner, *An Iranian Town in Transition. A Social and Economic History of the Elites of Tabriz, 1747-1848*, Wiesbaden: Harrassowits Verlag, 2000, pp. 81-82, 122-126, 224-228, 252.

5 The most important Shaykhī Kirmānī treatise concerning the rejection of any political interpretation or ideologization of Shi'ism is certainly the *Siyāsat-i mudun* of 'Abd al-Riḍā Khān Ibrāhīmī (d. 1979) composed in 1972. See Hermann, "Political Quietism in Contemporary Shī'ism: A Study of the *Siyāsat-i mudun* of the Shaykhī Kirmānī Master 'Abd al-Riḍā Khān Ibrāhīmī," *Studia Islamica*, vol. 109-2 (2014), pp. 274-302.

wards, *uṣūlī* and *akhbārī* trends acknowledge five religious principles (*uṣūl-i dīn*): *tawḥīd* (divine unity); *nubuwwat* (the cycle of prophecy); *imāmat* (the cycle of *imāmat*); *'adl* (justice); and *ma'ād* (resurrection). In Shaykhī Kirmānī doctrine, however, only the first three (namely *tawḥīd*, *nubuwwat*, and *imāmat*) are considered *uṣūl*, and to these principles is added a fourth pillar, the *rukn-i rābi'*.[6] This fourth pillar has to do with faith in a hidden Shi'i elite, on the same basis as the Twelfth Imām. This ideal community is hierarchic and entails a perfect Shi'a in direct communication with the Hidden Imām, the *nāṭiq-i wāḥid* (sole speaker), also called *bāb* (door); representatives called *nuqabā* (leaders or guides; singular *naqīb*); and the *nujabā* (nobles; singular *najīb*). These three categories of Shi'as are hidden, in the same way as the Twelfth Imām, and each member of this hidden elite is known only to those in the rank immediately below them. Below the *nujabā* are the ulemas, who can also be called *shakhṣ-i thiqa* (trustworthy men), terminology that can also be found in *Ijtihād wa taqlīd*.[7] The ulemas, unlike the rank just above them, are not hidden and are considered "visible evidence" (*ḥujjat-i ẓāhir*) of God. At the base of this spiritual hierarchy is the community of believers (*mu'min*), who make up only a small minority of all Muslims or Shi'as. These are also called "brothers" (*ikhwān* in Arabic or *barādarān* in Persian).[8] For Muḥammad Karīm Khān and his successors, the existence and the roles of the *nuqabā* and the *nujabā* are explicit in the Qur'ān and the *ḥadīth*.[9] There are always fewer of the *nuqabā* than of the *nujabā*, and they intervene in the affairs of the world in a hidden fashion.[10] The *nujabā* are basically in the midst of humanity, and their job is to com-

---

6 On the arguments of the Shaykhī Kirmānī that aim to show that the *rukn-i rābi'* is one of the *uṣūl-i dīn* and that *'adl* (justice) and *ma'ād* (resurrection) are *furū'-i dīn* (derived from religion), see Muḥammad Karīm Khān, "Risāla-yi jawāb-i shakhṣ-i Iṣfahānī," *Majma' al-rasā'il (15)*, Kerman: Sa'ādat, 1380/1961-62, pp. 1-107, esp. pp. 52-74; Muḥammad Karīm Khān, "Risāla-yi jawāb-i Sipahdār," *Majma' al-rasā'il-i fārsī (1)*, Kerman: Sa'ādat, 1386/1966-67, pp. 244-254, esp. pp. 250-253; Muḥammad Khān, *Mū'iẓa-yi 'aqāyid*, Kerman: Sa'ādat, 1348sh./1969-70; Muḥammad Khān, *Wasīla al-nijāt*, Kerman: Sa'ādat, 1383/1963-64, pp. 217-222; and Abū al-Qāsim Khān Ibrāhīmī, *Risāla-yi falsafiyya dar jawāb-i sū'ālāt-i jināb-i mustaṭāb-i Āqā-yi Falsafī-yi Wā'iẓ*, Kerman: Sa'ādat, 1350sh./1971-72, pp. 185-221.

7 On the doctrine of the fourth pillar in Shaykhī Kirmānī writings, see Muḥammad Karīm Khān, *Irshād al-'awāmm*, Kerman: Sa'ādat, 1354-55sh./1975-77; Muḥammad Karīm Khān, *Rukn-i rābi'*, Kerman: Sa'ādat, 1368/1948-49; Muḥammad Karīm Khān, *Tawḥīd, nubuwwa, imāma, shī'a*, Tabriz: ed. Litho, 1310/1892-93; and 'Abd al-Riḍā Khān Ibrāhīmī, *Dūstī-yi dūstān*, Kerman: Sa'ādat, 1400/1979-80. For an analysis of *rukn-i rābi'*, see Mohammad Ali Amir-Moezzi, "An Absence Filled with Presences: Shaykhiyya Hermeneutics of the Occultation," in Mohammad Ali Amir-Moezzi, *The Spirituality of Shi'i Islam*, London: I.B. Tauris, 2011, pp. 461-485; Henry Corbin, *En Islam iranien. Aspects spirituels et philosophiques*, Vol. IV, Paris: Gallimard, 1971, pp. 274-286.

8 Muḥammad Karīm Khān Kirmānī, *Irshād al-'awāmm*, Vol. IV, pp. 427-508.

9 See Muḥammad Karīm Khān, *Irshād al-'awāmm*, Vol. IV, pp. 176-207. See also Muḥammad Khān, "Risāla-yi jawāb-i Nawwāb Mīrzā Sayyid 'Alī Yazdī," *Majma' al-rasā'il-i fārsī (3)*, Kerman: Sa'ādat, 1388/1968-69, pp. 272-330.

10 Within the *ḥadīth* there are several variations on the number of *nuqabā* and *nujabā*. But Muḥammad Karīm Khān most often speaks of 12 *nuqabā* and 70 *nujabā*. See Muḥammad Karīm Khān, *Irshād al-'awāmm*, Vol. IV, pp. 371-373; Muḥammad Karīm Khān, *Sī faṣl dar*

municate the knowledge of the Imams to the elite among the believers.[11] Like the *nuqabā*, they are divided into two groups: the *nujabā-yi kullī* (perfect nobles) and *nujabā-yi juz'ī* (incomplete nobles).[12] When a *naqīb* dies, he is immediately replaced by one of the *nujabā*.[13] The *nuqabā* and the *nujabā*, more than any other members of the spiritual elite, are responsible for a bond between the Imām of the Time and believers; they also symbolize the status of the perfect human being (*insān-i kāmil*).[14] In addition, they make it possible for the original bond with the Imām of the Time to continue in a period dominated by ignorance (*jahl*) and the "people of ignorance" (*ahl-i jahl*). For the Shaykhī Kirmānīs, this division of Islam into four pillars makes Shi'ism the most perfect religion of mystical love. The first pillar represents love for God (represented by *tawḥīd*); the second, love for the prophets (*nubuwwat*); the third, love for the Imams (*imāmat*); and the fourth, finally, love for the Shi'as (*rukn-i rābi'*). This sentiment is illustrated by the translation of a famous *ḥadīth* by the Imām 'Alī on this subject: "Whoever loves God loves the Prophet. Whoever loves the Prophet loves us (the Imams). Whoever loves us (the Imams) loves the Shi'as, because the Prophet, ourselves, and the Shi'as are all of one and the same natural disposition (*ṭīnat*) and we are all in Paradise."[15]

---

jawāb-i īrādat-i ba'ḍ-i mūridīn bar silsila-yi jalīla-yi shaykhiyya, Kerman: Sa'ādat, 1368/1948-49, pp. 102-103.

11 See, in particular, Muḥammad Karīm Khān, *Irshād al-'awāmm*, Vol. IV, pp. 252-273.

12 See, in particular, 'Abd al-Riḍā Khān Ibrāhīmī, *Dūstī-yi dūstān*, pp. 183-198.

13 See Muḥammad Khān, "Risāla-yi jawāb-i Mīrzā Riḍā'ī Jandaqī," *Majma' al-rasā'il-i fārsī (3)*, pp. 2-14, especially pp. 10-14.

14 See Muḥammad Khān, "Risāla-yi jawāb-i sū'ālāt-i ba'ḍī az ma'rifat-i shakhṣ-i kāmil," *Majma' al-rasā'il-i fārsī (3)*, pp. 332-352.

15 'Abd al-Riḍā Khān Ibrāhīmī, *Siyāsat-i mudun*, Kerman: Sa'ādat, 1350sh./1971-72, p. 132.

II. The Life and Works of Abū al-Qāsim Khān Ibrāhīmī

Abū al-Qāsim Khān was born in 1314/1897 and took over the leadership of the Shaykhī Kirmānī school upon the death of his father, Zayn al-ʿĀbidīn Khān Kirmānī (d. 1360/1941). Abū al-Qāsim Khān had begun his religious studies in childhood, studying with various members of the school, including his older brother, Muḥammad Jawād;[1] later, he studied with his father, who conferred a general *ijāza* (permission to teach) on him in 1348/1930.[2] While Abū al-Qāsim Khān was the head of the school, he dedicated himself in particular to drawing up the first catalogue of the works of the masters, the *Fihrist-i kutub-i mashāyikh-i ʿiẓām*.[3] Only the works of the masters are included here and not those of their students. The catalogue's long introduction can be seen as the first history of the school written by a Shaykhī master. Abū al-Qāsim Khān also devoted a large part of his time to teaching at the Ibrāhīmiyya madrasa.[4] In addition, he played a central role in the founding of the school's publishing house, Saʿādat, which published, from 1960 to 1970, a great deal of the works of the school's masters and, in particular, of its two co-founders.

Abū al-Qāsim Khān himself is the author of twenty-three treatises, which is significantly less than what his predecessors wrote. *Ijtihād wa taqlīd* is certainly one of his most important treatises; *Risāla-yi tanzīh al-awliyyāʾ* (1265/1946) and *Risāla-yi falsafiyya* should also be mentioned. Of these last two, the first, *Risāla-yi tanzīh al-awliyyā'*, is a defense of *Irshād al-ʿawāmm*, which is almost certainly Muḥammad Karīm Khān's major work. *Risāla-yi falsafiyya* is an answer to several questions about Shaykhī doctrine. In addition, we should note that *Ijtihād wa taqlīd* was not the only treatise in which Abū al-Qāsim Khān addressed *fiqh*. In his *Nihāya* he also returned to the science of the *uṣūl-i dīn* and the *furūʿ-i dīn*.

Abū al-Qāsim Khān died during a pilgrimage to Mashhad in 1969 and was buried there. The local ulemas objected to his funeral, which is a characteristic example of the opposition that he suffered throughout his life. The publication of his *Ijtihād wa taqlīd* in 1362/1943, shortly after his accession to the leadership of the school, appears to have drawn the ire of some clerics; a number of defamatory and virulently anti-Shaykhī treatises were written during his leadership of the

---

1 Mahdī Bāmdād, *Sharḥ-i hāl-i rijāl-i Īrān dar qarn-i 12, 13, 14 hijrī*, Vol. VI, Tehran: Zawār, 1347-1353sh./1968-1975, pp. 31-32.

2 MacEoin, "Abu'l-Qāsem Khan Ebrāhīmī," *Encyclopaedia Iranica*, vol. I, 1985, pp. 363-364.

3 Abū al-Qāsim Khān Ibrāhīmī, *Fihrist-i kutub.*

4 Regarding the centrality of the Ibrāhīmiyya School for the Shaykhī community of Kerman, see Denis Hermann and Omid Rezai, "Le rôle du *vaqf* dans la formation de la communauté *shaykhī kermānī* à l'époque qājār (1259-1324/1843-1906)," *Studia Iranica*, vol. 36-1 (2007), pp. 87-131.

school. The most notable of these may be Shaykh Muḥammad Khāliṣī Kāẓimī (d. 1963)'s *Kitāb-i khurāfāt-i shaykhiyya wa kufriyyat-i Irshād al-'awāmm yā dasā'is-i kishīshān dar Īrān* [The Superstitions of the Shaykhīs and the Blasphemies of the *Irshād al-'awāmm*, or the Conspiracies of the Christian Priests in Iran]. This is one of the most violent of the anti-Shaykhī works, which was, incidentally, denounced by several of the most recognized and highest *uṣūlī* authorities of the time.[5] In this treatise, the author unleashed an array of calumnies against the co-founders of the Shaykhī school. He claimed to have established an intrinsic link between Shaykhism and Babism, asserting that Shaykh Aḥmad al-Aḥsā'ī and Sayyid Kāẓim Rashtī were British and Russian spies and priests who had managed to disguise their identity in order to destroy Islam from the inside by founding the Shaykhī school.[6] He even alleged that the Shaykhīs had some responsibility for all of the colonial wars that had been waged in the Muslim world since the nineteenth century,[7] going as far as to say that they had a role in the Zionist movement and in the creation of the state of Israel.[8]

Abū al-Qāsim Khān did not write any one specific treatise in response to the *Kitāb-i khurāfāt-i shaykhiyya*, but in his *Shikāyatnāma* [Complaint], he returned to the denunciations to which the Shaykhīs had been subject during this period.[9] In his introduction to the catalogue of the works of the masters of the school, he also indicated that he had been threatened by Shaykh Muḥammad Khāliṣī Kāẓimī and his disciples or henchmen during a pilgrimage to Iraq. These men had tried to constrain Abū al-Qāsim Khān movements within the country and to prevent him from getting to the *'atabāt*.[10] In his *Shikāyatnāma*, therefore, Abū al-Qāsim Khān called on the high clergy, asking them how they could allow preachers (*ahl-i minbar*) who were often ignorant about Shaykhism to spread such hatred throughout the mosques all over the country.[11] He emphasized, in particular, the two-facedness of these preachers, who presented themselves elsewhere as champions of Pan-Islamism. Given this, he asked ironically why these clerics had not gone so far as to excommunicate the Sunnis for not recognizing the Imamate, since they called the Shaykhīs infidels for the nuances of their interpretation of the return of the physical body at the resurrection (*ma'ād-i jismānī*) and the physical ascension (*mi'rāj-i jismānī*) of the Prophet.[12]

---

5 See the preface of the response by the Shaykhī Tabrīzī scholar Ghulām Ḥusayn Mu'tamad al-Islām, *Kalimahī az hizār... dar radd-i nashriyya-yi mazdūrān-i isti'mār*, n.p, n.d.

6 Shaykh Muḥammad Khāliṣī Kāẓimī, *Kitāb-i khurāfāt-i shaykhiyya wa kufriyyat-i irshād al-'awāmm yā dasā'is-i kishīshān dar Īrān*, n.p, 1367/1947-48, pp. 15-16, 19-20.

7 Ibid., pp. 7, 135.

8 Ibid., p. 36.

9 Abū al-Qāsim Khān Ibrāhīmī, *Shikāyatnāma*, Kerman: Sa'ādat, n.d.

10 Abū al-Qāsim Khān Ibrāhīmī, *Fihrist-i kutub*, notes to pp. 17-24.

11 Abū al-Qāsim Khān Ibrāhīmī, *Shikāyatnāma*, pp. 2-5, 24-25, 28, 30-31.

12 Ibid., pp. 29-30.

The Structure of Ijtihād wa taqlīd

Ijtihād wa taqlīd was first written and published in Arabic, and then translated into Persian. The present essay deals with the Persian version.[13] The work, which consists of more than 250 pages, is made up of two chapters and an appendix. The first chapter is entitled *Dar manshā-yi ijtihād wa taqlīd* [On the Origins of *ijtihād* and of *taqlīd*]; the second bears the title *Dar taqlīd-i mayyit* [On the Imitation of a Dead Man]. The appendix, finally, consisting of twenty-some pages, deals with the *nāṭiq-i wāḥid.* This is not unusual; it is common in Shaykhī Kirmānī literature for a treatise whose central themes do not deal with the fourth pillar to end with amplifications on the doctrine of the *rukn-i rābi'*. In returning to the *nāṭiq-i wāḥid* in the appendix, Abū al-Qāsim Khān wishes to demonstrate that it is only in taking the doctrine of the *rukn-i rābi'* into account that it is possible to fully understand the problems raised by *ijtihād* and *taqlīd* in Shi'i Islam.

On several occasions, Abū al-Qāsim Khān made a point of explaining why it was that he wrote this treatise in a straightforward style and in contemporary Persian. He said that he wanted to address the Muslim masses, in order to solve the problems and errors that seem evident to him. He also stated that the subject matter of the treatise is, finally, very simple for anyone who possesses "primordial faith" and that it would henceforth not be necessary to have recourse to a complicated dialectic: "The truth of our argumentation is self-evident here and it is not therefore necessary to use a very elaborate argumentation"[14] and again "That is the whole problem. Who is the person who can claim that as long as his reasoning is based on logic he will always arrive at the truth (*ḥaqīqat*)? ... We feel that it is necessary to repeat this principle again and again, clearly, so that the masses (*'awāmm*) will understand."[15] Abū al-Qāsim Khān declares that it is, in fact, his duty to express himself clearly, while at the same time being very aware that he is taking risks by acting in this way. He asserts at various points that he hopes that these questions will be understood by the Shi'as from now on.[16] Connecting the origins of *ijtihād* with Sunnism, he thus indicates to the Shi'as that they no longer have any reason to fear the Sunnis as they did in centuries past, and that they can therefore openly proclaim their rejection of this *fiqh*.

---

13 Abū al-Qāsim Khān Ibrāhīmī, *Ijtihād wa taqlīd*, Kerman: Sa'ādat, 1362/1943-44.
14 Ibid., p. 46.
15 Ibid., p. 72.
16 Ibid., p. 88.

III. What Is the Legacy of Akhbarism in Shaykhī Doctrine?

Even though there was no Shaykhī master before Abū al-Qāsim Khān who had written such an important work dealing explicitly with the earlier divisions within the Shi'i community between the *uṣūlī* and *akhbārī* currents, these questions had nevertheless of course been addressed in their writings.

If we limit ourselves to defining the essence of the *akhbārī* movement, embodied in Muḥammad Amīn al-Astarābādī starting in the middle of the eleventh/seventeenth century, as a rejection of *ijtihād*, of the idea of the "consensus of the majority of the Shi'i community" (*ijmā' al-firqa*),[1] and a greater attachment to the *ḥadīth*, then Shaykhism would appear to be the heir of that movement at a time when Akhbarism is in decline following the success it had during the twelfth/eighteenth century and the death of Shaykh Yūsuf Baḥrānī in 1186/1772.[2] And yet, there were nevertheless Shi'i ulemas who continued to profess Akhbarism during the nineteenth and twentieth centuries, particularly in Bahrain, which has remained a hub of Akhbarism, as has India.[3] Indeed, Akhbarism has certainly had a stronger impact than Shaykhism on the intellectual history of Shi'ism, be-

1 On this idea see Stewart in *Islamic Legal Orthodoxy*, pp. 159-160, 176.

2 Muḥammad Amīn Astarābādī was mainly responsible for the *akhbārī* renewal during the Safavid period. A list of the most important *akhbārī* ulemas of the seventeenth and eighteenth centuries would also include Muḥsin Fayḍ al-Kāshānī (d. 1091/1680), Mīrzā Muḥammad Nayshābūrī (d. 1233/1818), Qāḍī Sa'īd Qumī (d. 1103/1691), al-Ḥurr al-'Āmilī (d. 1099/1687-88), Ni'matullāh al-Jazā'irī (d. 1112/1700-01), and 'Abd Allāh al-Samahījī (d. 1135/1722-23). On the conditions that led to the *akhbārī* renewal and to its peak in the *'atabāt* from the end of the Safavid era to the Zand period, see Gleave, *Scripturalist Islam*, pp. 140-176; Idem, *Inevitable Doubt: Two Theories of Shī'ī Jurisprudence*, Leiden: Brill, 2000; Idem, "Akhbārī Shī'ī Uṣūl al-Fiqh and the Juristic Theory of Yūsuf b. Aḥmad al-Baḥrānī," in Robert Gleave and Eugenia Kermeli (ed.), *Islamic Law, Theory and Practice*, London: I.B. Tauris, 1997, pp. 24-48; Idem, "The Akhbārī-Usūlī Dispute in Tabaqat literature: An Analysis of the Biographies of Yūsuf al-Bahrānī and Muhammad Bāqir al-Bihbihānī," *Jusur*, vol. 10 (1994), pp. 79-109; Stewart, "The Genesis of the Akhbari Revival," in Michel Mazzaoui (ed.), *Safavid Iran and her Neighbors*, Salt Lake City: University of Utah Press, 2003, pp. 169-193; Idem, "The Humor of the Scholars: The Autobiography of Ni'mat Allah al-Jaza'iri (d. 1112/1701)," *Iranian Studies*, vol. 22/4 (1989), pp. 47-81; Andrew Newman, "The Nature of the Akhbārī/Uṣūlī dispute in Late-Safawid Iran. Part 1: 'Abdallāh al-Samāhijī's 'Munyat al-mumārisīn'," *Bulletin of the School of Oriental and African Studies*, vol. 55/1 (1992), pp. 22-52; Idem, "The nature of the Akhbārī/Uṣūlī dispute in Late-Safawid Iran. Part 2: The conflict reassessed," *Bulletin of the School of Oriental and African Studies*, vol. 55/2 (1992), pp. 250-262; Cole, "Shi'i Clerics in Iraq and Iran, 1722-1780: The Akhbari-Usuli Conflict Reconsidered," *Iranian Studies*, vol. 18/1 (1985), pp. 3-33.

3 On the *akhbārī* community that was established in Hyderabad at the end of the 1970s by Mawlānā Riḍā ud-Dīn Ḥaydar, see Toby M. Howarth, *The Twelver Shi'a as a Muslim Minority in India. Pulpit of Tears*, London: Routledge, 2005. See also the community's own website: www.akhbari.org (accessed in February 2015).

cause the attitude of the seventeenth- and eighteenth-century *akhbārī* authors undeniably created a great stir in the scholarship of *ḥadīth* and of *'ilm al-rijāl* (literally "the science of men," here referring to those who transmit *ḥadīth*s). As for realms other than *fiqh* and the central attachment to *ḥadīth*, however, it is difficult to establish any obvious connections between Akhbarism and Shaykhism, given that the positions of the *akhbārī* ulemas vary greatly. Thus, the Shaykhī hermeneutics of the Qur'ān and of the *ḥadīth* might well be different from that of the Akhbārī in spite of their shared rejection of a reliance on *'aql* or on conjectures (*ẓann*).[4] Nevertheless, like the Akhbārīs, the Shaykhī Kirmānīs refused to establish a categorization of *ḥadīth*s. As a result, they were criticized for referring to *ḥadīth* that their adversaries considered weak (*ḍā'if*); to this they retorted that neither God nor the Prophet had ever established any criteria on this subject.[5] The refutation of Sufism, which is shared by all branches of Shaykhism, is again something that is not characteristic of Akhbarism per se; it is shared only by some of the *akhbārī* ulemas.[6] And finally, the Shaykhī Kirmānīs subscribe to the thesis of the falsification of the Qur'ān (*taḥrīf al-Qur'ān*); as a result, they do not consider the Qur'ān that is known today among Muslims to be the one that was revealed to the Prophet Muḥammad. But even though some *akhbārī* authors share this conception, it would be a mistake to see in this an obvious similarity between Akhbarism and Shaykhism, because this principle was not systematically shared by all *akhbārī*

---

4 Gleave has made a survey of the very varied doctrinal positions of the *akhbārī* authors, in particular as they concern Qur'anic hermeneutics (*Scripturalist Islam*, pp. 216-244, 268-296). On the subject of the scholarship of commentary and exegesis in Akhbarism, see also Lawson, "Akhbari Shi'i approaches to tafsir," in Gerald Richard Hawting and Abdul-Kader A. Shareef (ed.), *Approaches to the Quran*, London: Routledge, 1993, pp. 173-210; and Lawson, "Exegesis. vi: In Akbārī and Post-Safavid Esoteric Shi'ism," *Encyclopaedia Iranica*, vol. X, 1999, pp. 123-125. There have not been any studies on the scholarship of *tafsīr* among the Shaykhī Kirmānīs, but they composed numerous Qur'anic or *ḥadīth* commentaries reflecting their hermeneutic approach to the sacred texts of Islam. By Muḥammad Karīm Khān, see *Īqān*; *Tafsīr-i sūra-yi hijrāt*; *Taqwīm al-lisān*; *Ḥāshiyya-yi Qur'ān*; *Risāla dar rasm al-khaṭṭ-i Qur'ān*; *Risāla dar sharḥ-i ḥadīth-i marvī dar kāfī*; *Fā'yida-yi mukhtiṣara*; *Risāla-yi jawāb-i Āqā-yi Mīrzā Luṭf 'Alī*; *Risāla dar jawāb-i sā'ilī az jam' bayn-i āyah yaūma kān*; *Risāla dar jawāb az ma'anī-yi ḥadīth-i nabawī*; *Risāla fī sharḥ-i du'ā al-saḥr*; *Muqtal*; *Ta'wīl al-ḥadīth fī 'ilm al-rūyā*; *Sharḥ-i ḥadīth al-faḍīla*; and *Sharḥ-i ḥadīth al-ma'rifat ba l-nūrāniyya*; by Muḥammad Khān, see *Risāla dar tafsīr-i āya anā 'arḍnā al-āmānat*; *Risāla dar tafsīr-i sūra-yi mubāraka-yi 'ankabūt*; *Risāla dar tafsīr-i sūra-yi fajr wa kawthar*; *Risāla dar tafsīr-i sūra-yi mubāraka-yi qadr*; *Risāla dar jawāb-i Ḥājj Muḥammad Ṣādiq Khān*; and *Risāla dar jawāb-i ba'ḍ-i ajilā-yi Yazd*; by Zayn al-'Ābidīn Khān Kirmānī, see *Fā'yidah dar jawāb-i Abū al-Ḥasan Khān*; *Risāla-yi jawāb-i Āqā Aḥmad darbāra-yi sūra-yi kawthar, wa tafsīr-i ān sūra*; *Tafsīr-i sūra-yi jum'a*; *Tafsīr-i sūra-yi munafiqīn*; *Risāla dar jawāb-i Jināb-i Āqā-yi Shaykh Ḥasan Sardravardī dar ma'anī wa tafsīr-i āya an awwal bayt waḍ' lalnās*; and *Risāla dar jawāb-i Āqā Sayyid 'Alī Khurāsānī az tafsīr-i āyāt.*

5 See Abū al-Qāsim Khān Ibrāhīmī, *Fihrist-i kutub*, p. 246.

6 On the refutation of Sufism or, on the other hand, the partial integration of Sufism among *akhbārī* scholars, see Gleave, "Scripturalist Sufism and Scripturalist Anti-Sufism: Theology and Mysticism amongst the Shi'i Akhbariyya," in Ayman Shihadeh (ed.), *Sufism and Theology*, Edinburgh: Edinburgh University Press, 2007, pp. 158-176.

authors and, what is more, was also upheld by some *uṣūlī*s as well as some Shi'i Sufi masters.[7]

Connections between Shaykh Aḥmad al-Aḥsā'ī and the akhbārī *Ulemas*

We do not have much information on the relationships that Shaykh Aḥmad al-Aḥsā'ī may have maintained with the last influential *akhbārī* ulemas. The eastern part of the Arabian Peninsula and the island of Bahrain mostly adhered to Akhbarism in the eighteenth century, and Shaykh Aḥmad al-Aḥsā'ī studied with several *akhbārī* scholars, including Shaykh Ḥusayn Al-'Aṣfūr, the nephew of Shaykh Yūsuf al-Baḥrānī, up through the end of the 1790s.[8] Nevertheless, we note that, for reasons that may be generational, the most important *ijāza* that Shaykh Aḥmad al-Aḥsā'ī procured came not from *akhbārī* ulemas but from *uṣūlī* scholars, which does not mean that he treated *ijtihād* as legitimate or that he identified with Usulism, which was quite dominant at the time.[9] In order to evaluate more precisely the positions of Shaykh Aḥmad al-Aḥsā'ī on *uṣūlī* and *akhbārī* theories, therefore, it would be necessary to undertake a systematic study of his writings on *fiqh*.[10]

Regardless, it would appear that Shaykh Aḥmad al-Aḥsā'ī was a very independent religious, and at this point it is very difficult to connect him with either Akhbarism or Usulism. His travels and constant moves make him a one-of-a-kind scholar, but we can point out that he never obtained a specific position such as that of judge (*qāḍī*), *shaykh al-islām*, or Imam of the Friday prayers (*imām-i jum'a*). It would be reasonable to believe that in fact he never attempted to obtain such a

---

7 Muḥammad Khān returned to this subject in *Ḥusām al-dīn dar ithbāt-i taḥrīf-i Tawrāh wa Anjīl*, Kerman: Sa'ādat, 1353sh./1974-75. On the position of *akhbārī* ulemas on the authenticity of the Qur'ān, see Lawson, "Note for the Study of a 'Shi'i' Qur'ān," *Journal of Semitic Studies*, vol. 36 (1991), pp. 279-295; Gleave, *Scripturalist Islam*, pp. 218-219. For an introduction to the history of the view of the Imamite ulemas on the question of the *taḥrīf al-Qu'rān* (falsification of the Qur'ān) see Mohammad Ali Amir-Moezzi and Etan Kohlberg, "Révélation et falsification. Introduction à l'édition du *Kitāb al-Qirā'āt* d'*Al-Sayyārī*," *Journal Asiatique*, vol. 293/2 (2005), pp. 663-722; Rainer Brunner, "La question de la falsification du Coran dans l'exégèse chiite duodécimaine," *Arabica*, vol. 52/1 (2005), pp. 1-42.

8 See Cole, "Rival Empires of Trade and Imami Shī'ism in Eastern Arabia, 1300-1800," *International Journal of Middle Eastern Studies*, vol. 19 (1987), pp. 177-204, at p. 196.

9 It is without a doubt Sayyid Muḥammad Mahdī Baḥr al-'Ulūm (d. 1212/1797-98) who granted him his most important *ijāza*. Baḥr al-'Ulūm, incidentally, had himself received an *ijāza* from the *akhbārī* ulema Yūsuf al-Baḥrānī (see Gleave, "The *Ijāza* from Yūsuf al-Baḥrānī (d. 1186/1772) to Sayyid Muḥammad Mahdī Baḥr al-'Ulūm (d. 1212/1797-98)," *Iran*, vol. 32 (1994), pp. 115-123). See the passages on Sayyid Baḥr al-'Ulūm in Sayyid Kāẓim Rashtī, *Dalīl al-mutaḥayyirīn*, (translated from Arabic into Persian by Zayn al-'Ābidīn Ibrāhīmī), Kerman: Sa'ādat, n.d, pp. 47-50; Muḥammad Karīm Khān, *Hidāyat al-ṭālibīn*, Kerman: Sa'ādat, 1380/1960-61, pp. 50, 56-57; and Muḥammad Khān, *Risāla-yi Bihbahāniyya*, pp. 10-24. On the status of Shaykh Aḥmad al-Aḥsā'ī in *uṣūlī* works see Cole, "Shaikh Ahmad al-Ahsa'i on the sources of religious authority."

10 Abū al-Qāsim Khān Ibrāhīmī, *Fihrist-i kutub*, pp. 309-314.

post, which would indicate that he was definitely circumspect about the socio-religious role of the *uṣūlī* clerics.

In addition, it is important to emphasize the fact that the Shaykhī Kirmānīs, like the *akhbārīs*, naturally gave a central place to the study of *ḥadīth* in their teaching.[11] The Kirmānī masters of the nineteenth century also, incidentally, composed several important compilations of *ḥadīths*, at the very moment in which that intellectual tradition was in massive decline.[12]

The Position of the Shaykhīs within the Intellectual History of Shi'ism

The Shaykhī Kirmānī masters rarely referred to literature that predated Shaykh Aḥmad al-Aḥsā'ī. In this way, they invited their followers to look first to the works of the Shaykhī masters and, in general, to regard the past with a critical eye. This brings us back to the many pages dedicated by the Shaykhī Kirmānī masters and, in particular, Muḥammad Karīm Khān, to justifying the late emergence of the Shaykhī school, which has often been presented as an indication of the maturation of Shi'i thought. They believed that following the Occultation (329/940-41), there was never more than a handful of scholars who were carrying on the message of the Imams, while many of the influential clerics were distorting Shi'i doctrine. This is also a natural process within Shi'ism, given its initiatory and minoritarian nature. The teachings of Shaykh Aḥmad al-Aḥsā'ī, then, represent a sort of break within the intellectual history of Shi'ism. For the Shaykhīs, he was the one who rejected past errors and put forth Imami doctrine while staying true to the revealed texts and the teaching of the infallibles (*ma'ṣūm*), without trying to drag Shi'ism into division (*fitna*).[13] The role of Shaykh Aḥmad al-Aḥsā'ī's successors, then, is to keep tirelessly presenting the teaching of the Imams so that the revelation will gradually make sense to Muslims: "the truth, by the grace of God, always reveals itself and discloses itself more every day. Very soon there will come a day when, if God wills it, all Muslims will know and understand that the scholarship of the great Shaykh [Aḥmad al-Aḥsā'ī] is true from every point of view and from what lazy slumber he

---

11 On the Shaykhīs' fundamental interest in *ḥadīth* and *akhbār* see Corbin, *En islam iranien*, vol. IV, pp. 257-262. As a general rule, the books that were bought and published through the institution of the *waqf* in the *uṣūlī* context had much less to do with *ḥadīth*. See 'Alī Riḍā Mīrzā Muḥammad, who gives the list of the works that were made into *waqf* for the theological students at the Maḥmūdiyya school in Tehran, "Waqfnāma-yi masjid-i madrasa-yi maḥmūdiyya-yi Tihrān," *Mīrāth-i jāwīdān*, vol. 29 (1379sh./2000-01), pp. 83-114, especially pp. 99-100; 'Imād al-Dīn Shaykh al-Ḥukamā'ī, "Masjid-i madrasa-yi mi'mārbāshī-yi Tihrān," *Mīrāth-i jāwīdān*, vol. 37 (1381sh./2002-03), pp. 25-32; Idem, "Waqfnāma-yi masjid-i madrasa-yi sipahsālār-i qadīr," *Mīrāth-i jāwīdān*, vol. 33-34 (1380sh./2001-02), pp. 121-132.

12 By Muḥammad Karīm Khān, see *Faḍl al-khiṭāb*; *Faḍl al-khiṭāb-i ṣaghīr*; and *Muqtal*; by Muḥammad Khān, see *Kitāb al-mubīn*; and *Muntakhab*.

13 In particular, see Muḥammad Khān, "Risāla dar jawāb-i iekī az rufaqā'i Nā'īnī," *Majma' al-rasā'il-i fārsī dar radd-i īrādāt (4)*, Kerman: Sa'ādat, 1351sh./1972-73, p. 23; and Abū al-Qāsim Khān Ibrāhīmī, *Risāla-yi falsafiyya*, pp. 256-257.

has woken them."[14] And yet, we note that it is primarily the experts on *ḥadīth*, the *muḥaddithīn*, often associated with Akhbarism from the Safavid era on, who are respected and taken into consideration by the Shaykhī Kirmānīs. Kulaynī (d. 328-329/939-41),[15] Ibn Babūya (d. 380-81/991),[16] al-Ḥurr al-ʿĀmilī (d. 1099/1688),[17] and Muḥammad Bāqir Majlisī (d. 1111/1699-1700)[18] come to mind. The Shaykhī Kirmānī masters did not make any basic criticisms of Akhbarism. They did, however, express regret that some *akhbārī* scholars had allowed themselves to be drawn into conjectures (*ẓann*) and had upheld concepts or rulings (*ḥukm*) that were not verified or confirmed by the Qur'ān or the *ḥadīth*. This in turn implies that their scholarship is not ultimately based on formal elements (*qaṭʿī*) and can therefore no longer constitute a certainty (*yaqīn*). Of course, this criticism has wide-ranging consequences, because what the *akhbārī* scholars accused the *uṣūlī* ulemas of was precisely not sticking closely enough to the scriptural sources. But these comments remained general, and it was rare for a particular scholar to be named. If Sayyid Kāẓim Rashtī was unhappy about differences which set one *akhbārī ʿalim* against another, in particular, say, differences between Shaykh Yūsuf Baḥrānī and his son Shaykh Ḥusayn b. ʿAṣfūr, such criticisms remained minimal.[19] In fact, elsewhere, Muḥammad Khān Kirmānī (d. 1324/1906) [Muḥammad Khān], the fourth shaykhī Kirmānī master, recognized Shaykh Yūsuf Baḥrānī as a major Shiʿi scholar.[20] In addition, we find these comments in works whose purpose is to defend the legal approaches of the *akhbārīs* as opposed to those of the *uṣūlīs*.[21] At times, the desire of the Shaykhīs to convince those Shiʿas who were sensitive to the legal process of Akhbarism is clear. Abū al-Qāsim Khān, in fact, in his *Ijtihād va taqlīd*, affirms that the *akhbārī* scholars are only lacking a few elements that would allow them to possess certainty (*yaqīn*). In addition, Abū al-Qāsim Khān declares that "the principles of Akhbarism are a thousand times more solid than those of Usulism."[22] Muḥammad Karīm Khān, for his part, declared that Shaykh Aḥmad al-Aḥsā'ī completely rejected Usulism but not Akhbarism.

It would seem here that the Shaykhī Kirmānīs claim to have complicated the very literalist *akhbārī* approach, which Abū al-Qāsim Khān described in his treaty

---

14 Abū al-Qāsim Khān Ibrāhīmī, *Fihrist-i kutub*, p. 195.

15 See Muḥammad Karīm Khān, "Risāla dar jawāb-i īrādāt-i Mullā Ḥusayn ʿAlī Tūīsirkānī bar silsila-yi ʿilliyya," *Majmaʿ al-rasā'il (15)*, pp. 110-188: p. 140.

16 See Muḥammad Khān, *Risāla-yi ʿaqāyid-i shaykhiyya*, p. 27.

17 On this last *ʿalim*, see Gleave, "Scriptural Sufism," pp. 160-166.

18 See Sayyid Kāẓim Rashtī, *Dalīl al-mutaḥayyirīn*, p. 73; and Muḥammad Karīm Khān, "Risāla dar jawāb-i īrādāt-i Mullā Ḥusayn ʿAlī Tūīsirkānī bar silsila-yi ʿilliyya," p. 140.

19 Sayyid Kāẓim Rashtī, "Dar jawāb-i baʿḍ-i Ahl-i Iṣfahān," *Majmaʿ al-rasā'il (16)*, Kerman: Saʿādat, pp. 276-357: p. 294.

20 Muḥammad Khān, *Mawʿiẓah-yi ʿaqāyid*, Kerman: Saʿādat, p. 65.

21 See Sayyid Kāẓim Rashtī, "Risāla dar jawāb-i sā'ilī," in *Majmaʿ al-rasā'il (16)*, p. 183; Sayyid Kāẓim Rashtī, "Dar jawāb-i baʿḍ-i Ahl-i Iṣfahān," pp. 276-357; and Abū al-Qāsim Khān Ibrāhīmī, *Ijtihād wa taqlīd*, pp. 20-21, 60-61.

22 Abū al-Qāsim Khān Ibrāhīmī, *Ijtihād wa taqlīd*, p. 127.

as too "simplistic" (*sādigī*).[23] For him, it is the faith in the spiritual elite of the *rukn-i rābi'* and the "trustworthy men" (*shakhṣ-i thiqa*) that allows the Shi'as to rely, during the Occultation, on a certain knowledge (*yaqīn*).[24]

The rhetoric about the disfiguring of Shi'ism at the hands of the *uṣūlī* ulemas was, we should note, already very present in the writings of Muḥammad Karīm Khān and Muḥammad Khān. They also criticized the "legal principles" (*uṣūl-i fiqh*) of the *uṣūlī*s in several of their works that were not necessarily devoted to *fiqh*. For this, one can also consult the second chapter of *Hidāyat al-ṭālibīn*, completed by Muḥammad Karīm Khān in December of 1845,[25] in which he fearlessly asserted his rejection of *ijtihād* and of *taqlīd* based on the *mujtahid*. He did not hesitate to state that this amounted to changing and losing his religion, putting in its place the religion of an ordinary man, that of the *mujtahid*. His purpose here is to demonstrate, step by step, that it is his opponents who do not recognize the teaching of the Imams. He compares the speculative legal methods of the *mujtahid*s to the methods of the rabbis and openly accuses them of "lying" to believers. At the same time, he amasses citations of *ḥadīth*s on the topic of evil ulemas, who are presented as being the worst of beings, after Satan, Pharaoh, and Nimrod.[26] He also declares that every time the *uṣūlī*s hold a meeting to prove their right to *ijtihād*, the Shaykhī Kirmānīs will answer with another assembly, destined to prove the right of the highest authorities of the occult spiritual hierarchy to *ijtihād*: "Every time that you prove your *ijtihād* in your gatherings (*majlis*), as for us, we will organize other meetings at which we will prove its right [the right of the highest spiritual authority] to *ijtihād*."[27] Nevertheless, it is important to point out that if the Shaykhī Kirmānī masters denounced the usage and meaning given to *ijtihād* by the *uṣūlī mujtahid*s, they also, at the same time, proposed a reinterpretation of the concept. This was, in particular, the purpose of a few pages of *Ijtihād wa taqlīd*.[28]

---

23 Ibid., pp. 125-132.

24 Ibid., pp. 65-66, 141, 158-162, 169, 196, and 263-290.

25 Muḥammad Karīm Khān, *Hidāyat al-ṭālibīn*; see also Muḥammad Khān, "Risāla dar jawāb-i iekī az rufaqā'i Nā'īnī," p. 23.

26 Muḥammad Karīm Khān, *Hidāyat al-ṭālibīn*, pp. 97, 100.

27 Ibid., p. 140.

28 Abū al-Qāsim Khān Ibrāhīmī also comes back to this question in his *Shikāyatnāma*, pp. 78-81.

IV. A Study of *Ijtihād wa taqlīd*

A. The Meaning of the Word ijtihād

The common meaning given to the concept of *ijtihād*, in other words here the independent interpretive effort of a legal scholar for the purpose of arriving at a legal proposition in the absence of clear indications on the subject in the Qur'ān or in the *ḥadīth*, is rejected by Abū al-Qāsim Khān in the most explicit fashion possible, from the very beginning of his work: "The word *ijtihād* means a great effort, and for the *mujtahid*s this takes on the meaning of a considerable effort in order to obtain a conjectural religious sentence (*kushish-i bisyārī dar taḥṣīl-i ẓann ba ḥukm-i sharʿī*). That is to say that after a great effort, they believe that what they have produced on a particular subject is in fact the ruling of God and of the Prophet. Their decisions become, in practice, the ruling of God and of the Prophet, and they take on an obligatory character (*wājib*) for the imitators (*muqallid*) who are required to submit to them. And if someone does not follow the sentence of the *mujtahid* and rejects it, then his worship practices (*ʿibādat*) are invalid."[1] The *ijtihād* of the *mujtahid*, then, is above all regarded as a conjecture (*ẓann*). The text often calls it a "conjectural *ijtihād*." This gives rise to the pairing of the words *ijtihād-ẓann*. In addition, Abū al-Qāsim Khān reminds us that there are more than seventy Qur'anic verses and more than twelve hundred *ḥadīth*s that explicitly condemn the use of conjectures.[2] Such an action is forbidden (*ḥarām*) and regarded as a lie (*durūgh*): "The use of conjectures has been declared to be forbidden (*ḥarām*). It is the worst kind of lie."[3] Abū al-Qāsim Khān also defines this act as a blameworthy innovation and an invention (*ikhtirāʿ*) with dramatic consequences for Islam.[4] Thus, the word *ẓann* is also associated with the word "doubt" (*shakk*).[5] The use of conjectures, then, runs counter to one of the key concepts for all of Shaykhī Kirmānī argumentation, namely the need for certainties (*yaqīn*) and established beliefs (*qaṭīʿ*). Abū al-Qāsim Khān regularly returns to the necessity for every believer to arrive at certainties that will assure him of serenity and salvation (*nijāt*).[6] Nor is *ẓann* the only negative term that Abū al-Qāsim Khān connects with the *ijtihād* of the *mujtahid*. In the very first pages of the treatise, *ijtihād* is also connected with several other terms, remaining synonymous with them throughout the entire work. The first of these is belief

---

1 Abū al-Qāsim Khān Ibrāhīmī, *Ijtihād wa taqlīd*, p. 9.

2 The *akhbārī* scholar al-Samāhijī also mentioned these Qur'anic verses and these *ḥadīth*s, quoting some of them in his *Munyat al-mumārisīn*. See Newman, "The nature of the Akhbārī/Uṣūlī dispute in Late-Safawid Iran. Part 1," p. 39.

3 Abū al-Qāsim Khān Ibrāhīmī, *Ijtihād wa taqlīd*, p. 143.

4 Ibid., p. 219.

5 Ibid., p. 124.

6 Ibid., pp. 117-119, 123.

(*gumān*) without an established basis.[7] Here, then, it is a matter of indicating that the *ijtihād* of the *mujtahid* is a personal opinion, independent of the teaching of the Imams and possibly in fact contrary to that teaching: "There is no remaining doubt that at the time of the majestic Prophet (*payghambar-i buzurgavār*), *ijtihād* did not exist in the community (*ummat*) and there were no 'rules' (*qawā'id wa uṣūlī*) for issuing religious rulings (*ḥukm-i shar'ī*) on the basis of a simple belief (*gumān*). The community therefore obeyed everything that the Prophet commanded without asking how or why. The ruling of God revealed in the Qur'ān was that no-one compared himself to God or to his Prophet;"[8] "Making one's decisions on the basis of conjectures (*ẓann*), personal beliefs (*gumān*), or *ijtihād* is forbidden (*ḥarām*). All the corruptions (*fasād*) that we find in religion arise from these practices;"[9] "We cannot even manage to conceive anymore that a *mujtahid* would abstain from declaring that the *muqallid* should follow their own personal beliefs (*gumān*) in the practice of God's religion."[10]

Abū al-Qāsim Khān connects some other key technical terms of Sunni law with *ijtihād*. The first of these is the concept of "personal opinion" (*rā'y*). We will see that the *ijtihād* of the *mujtahid*s is considered to come from Sunnism and therefore to be foreign to Shi'ism and explicitly condemned by the Imams. Abū al-Qāsim Khān also refers to "analogical reasoning" (*qiyās*), which was condemned by Imām Ja'far Ṣādiq (d. 148/765) after Abū Ḥanīfa (d. 150/767) had called for its use.[11] Abū al-Qāsim Khān also says that the *ijtihād* of the *mujtahid*s comes from the air (*havā'ī*), that is to say from nowhere.[12] Thus, Abū al-Qāsim Khān regularly uses the following chain of word associations: *ijtihād-ẓann-gumān-rā'y-qiyās-havā'ī.*

B. The Notion of muqallid

Abū al-Qāsim Khān is a vehement critic of the division of the Shi'i community into two categories, namely the *mujtahid*s on one side and the *muqallid*s on the other. The *muqallid*s are those who are compelled according to *uṣūlī* doctrine to observe their *taqlīd* following a living *mujtahid.* Abū al-Qāsim Khān brings up this question in the very first sentence of the first chapter of *Ijtihād wa taqlīd.* He in no way, then, resorts to *taqiyya* (dissimulation of faith). He openly criticized the *uṣūlī* clergy, in spite of the dangers that they pose to the Shaykhī school and the members of its community. This is also another indication of the degree to which Abū al-Qāsim Khān desired that this work should be clear to everyone. Nevertheless, we shall see that, as with the concept of *ijtihād*, Abū al-Qāsim Khān does not reject

7 Ibid., p. 12.
8 Ibid., p. 12.
9 Ibid., p. 62.
10 Ibid., p. 65.
11 Ibid., pp. 26-27.
12 Ibid., p. 16.

the use of the terms *taqlīd* and *muqallid* but instead insists on giving them what he considers to be their original meaning. *Taqlīd* is allowed, and even obligatory, with respect to infallible Imams (*maʿṣūm*) and "trustworthy men" who do not, of course, practice *ijtihād-ẓann-gumān*. We have already pointed out that "trustworthy men" make up one of the categories of the fourth pillar. While the *akhbārī* scholars also legitimized complying with the teaching passed on by the ulemas who were faithful transmitters of the *ḥadīth*, they may not have insisted on this point as strongly as did the Shaykhīs.[13]

On this topic, here are some particularly explicit passages from *Ijtihād wa taqlīd*:

> How is it that Muslims could be so blind, deaf, and mute as to accept that men are divided into two categories, the *mujtahid*s and the *muqallid*s of the *mujtahid*s? How can they be willing to rely on the conjectures of the *mujtahid*s to establish the rulings of God's religion and how can they demand that we consider the conjecture of the *mujtahid*s as a "proof" (*ḥujjat*)? The *muqallid* is not even allowed to ask questions of the *mujtahid* and is required to accept the *mujtahid*'s opinions. How can they believe that these principles are those of established religion (*yaqīn*)? How is it that they believe that this is God's religion, and how can they believe that in respecting it they will obtain eternal Paradise tomorrow? ... Aren't these declarations [on the law of the *mujtahid*s and the division of the community into two categories] surprising? Wouldn't Muslims, after having heard this, wish to understand more of religion?[14]

From this point on, the *muqallid*s are presented as candid and simple beings, unthinkingly repeating the practices of their elders. Thus, they are sometimes called "poor ignorants" (*bīchāra-yi jāhil*), prisoners of the goodwill of the *mujtahid*s and manipulated by them:

> Why do some *mullā*s intervene to contradict the words of another *mullā*s when they have not even heard him? These are men with ambition, who are not men of science (*ahl-i ʿilm*) and, in fact, are do not even dress like men of science. The "poor ignorants" (*bīchāra-yi jāhil*) become their disciples with complete goodwill and believe that imitating one of them is like following the [Hidden] Imām. They believe that they are practicing *taqlīd* according to the Imām himself, whereas everything that such a *mullā* says is the result of his own personal opinion (*rā'y*) and of *ijtihād*. In no case is this a commandment of the Imams. For this reason, God has told us to rely on "trustworthy men" for what concerns religion. Understanding Shi'ism consists of assimilating the traditions of the Imams. Therefore, we must all rely on the *akhbār* and know those who take on the role of intermediary between the *akhbār* and men.[15]

We can see, therefore, that Abū al-Qāsim Khān heavily stresses the inconsistency of the division of the community into two groups, referring to the centrality of the doctrine of the fourth pillar. This lack of logic reveals the ignorance of the *uṣūlī*s, but also of the *akhbārī*s, as far as the *rukn-i rābiʿ* is concerned. Thus, it is their very understanding of the meaning of Shi'ism that is called into question in

---

13 See Newman, "The nature of the Akhbārī/Uṣūlī dispute in Late-Safawid Iran. Part 1," p. 41.
14 Abū al-Qāsim Khān Ibrāhīmī, *Ijtihād wa taqlīd*, pp. 65-66.
15 Ibid., p. 244.

a basic way, because the finality of religion (*gharaḍ-i dīn*) escapes them. And thus, Abū al-Qāsim Khān calls for the non-*mujtahid*s who have been condemned to the status of *muqallid*s to exert themselves to better understand Islam: "It is possible, then, for non-*mujtahid*s who have some command of Arabic to understand the rulings of the Prophet and to practice them. They can free themselves from *ijtihād* and acquire knowledge without having to rely on conjectures."[16] According to Abū al-Qāsim Khān, then, this division between *mujtahid*s and *muqallid*s maintains the ignorance of the masses and their passivity about initiating themselves into the teaching of the Imams contained in the corpus of sources that is made up by the *ḥadīth*:

> No one should look for a *mujtahid* in order to blindly practice *taqlīd* following him until he dies, without even understanding or knowing the origin of the rulings that he proclaimed. No one should look for a new *mujtahid* once the first one has died, even if the *mujtahid*s have declared that the *taqlīd* of a dead man was forbidden (*ḥarām*).[17]

Abū al-Qāsim Khān, then, supports the idea according to which a *muqallid* is forced to live a religious life that can bring him neither spiritual peace nor salvation (*nijāt*):

> Every sincere and devout Muslim (*muslim*) and believer (*mu'min*) who has been invited to embrace Islam and who presents himself as a faithful follower of the Prophet must know that his religion derives from the prophecy of the Prophet. He must understand that he has no right to interfere (*dikhālat*) in the religion of the Prophet and in his rulings, whether complete (*aḥkām-i kuliyya*) or partial (*aḥkām-i juziyya*). He cannot associate with the Prophet in what God has revealed to him because the religion and the revealed book of the Prophet present the entirety of the complete and partial rulings, the principles, and what is derived from them. No-one at all has been authorized to add or subtract anything from them. In forbidding the exercise of *ijtihād*, God and his Prophet have made everyone's life simpler and less burdensome (*rāḥat wa asūda*).[18]

Therefore, according to Abū al-Qāsim Khān, *ijtihād* causes corruption (*fasād*) because Muslims do not know which way to turn nor which *sharī'a* and religion to adopt:

> Why don't we all become *mujtahid*s? Then we will see how many *mujtahid*s there will be. Then we will all be able to issue fatwas and rulings. At that moment, we will see how many legal treatises are written and to what degree corruption (*fasād*) will develop. ... Then everyone will be able to use *ijtihād* and to issue fatwas and will, then, have his own religion, because he will not respect the fatwas issued by others. Nobody will pray behind other *mujtahid* anymore.[19] ... If we brought back the fatwas of the Imams this would not happen. ... All of these problems arise from *ijtihād*. That is what corrupts and weakens Muslims and Islam itself. ... When the *mujtahid* sees that his own imperfect rea-

16 Ibid., pp. 134-135.
17 Ibid., p. 234.
18 Ibid., p. 38.
19 We know that for the *uṣūlī*s, communal prayer is recommended from the moment when a *mujtahid* is present in the assembly and is leading the prayer.

son (*'aql-i nāqiṣ*) has now taken on the character of a ruling and that his inconsequential belief (*gumān-i bījā*) has now taken on the character of a proof (*ḥujjat*), four people who come from the stupid masses (*'awāmm-i aḥmaq*) will accept him and become his servants. This *mujtahid* will then no longer know his own limits and will claim to possess a status comparable to that of the Imam and the Prophet. And beyond that, he will want to see the simple people praying behind him and to have them be dependent on him. Every day he makes what is allowed forbidden and what is forbidden allowed. What is more, no-one has the right to question him because the *muqallid* may not know the reasons behind the judgments of the *mujtahid*.[20]

The *mujtahid*s are therefore being accused of using religion, regularly modifying the law and forcing Shi'i believers to submit to their authority. Abū al-Qāsim Khān considers this to be at the source of continual disturbances.[21] The practice of *ijtihād* can result in the issuance of illegitimate religious rulings, completely meaningless and contradicting each other. Abū al-Qāsim Khān even holds *ijtihād-ẓann* responsible for destroying the *sharī'a* that is at the basis of all cultures and civilizations, of human dignity and of honor (*nāmūs*). He also compares the methods of Usulism to those of rabbinical Judaism, concluding that the rabbis asked Jewish communities to practice *taqlīd* on the rabbis themselves rather than following the prophets. The *mujtahid*s, then, are accused of rendering the *ḥalāl ḥarām* (forbidding that which is allowed) and the *ḥarām ḥalāl* (allowing that which is forbidden)[22].

Abū al-Qāsim Khān regrets that the conjectures of the *mujtahid* have become a proof (*ḥujjat*) in the eyes of some people, thereby disturbing the religion and the cosmic order.[23] He also finds it deplorable that the hierarchization of the clergy over control of *ijtihād* should have the added flaw that it makes *fiqh* into the be-all and end-all of religious education. Given that, he also notes the weakening of the most important fields of religious studies, such as the initiation into the Qur'anic text and into *ḥadīth*.[24] According to him, the perpetual debate (*baḥth*) on questions of *fiqh* can therefore not help but result in controversies and conflicts.[25]

But one of the worst consequences of the use of *ijtihād* by the *uṣūlī mujtahid*s, according to Abū al-Qāsim Khān, remains the feeling of desolation that some believers can feel, no longer being able to distinguish between what comes from the divine ruling and what is nothing more than the personal opinion of the *mujtahid*. Thus, in evoking the differences between the *mujtahid*s, Abū al-Qāsim Khān asks his reader whether it is God who wished there to be divergences within the law or whether it is the *mujtahid*s who invented them: "Is it God who ordained these differences and they did obey his ruling, or did God forbid these divergences but

20 Abū al-Qāsim Khān Ibrāhīmī, *Ijtihād wa taqlīd*, pp. 75-76.
21 Ibid., p. 153.
22 Ibid., pp. 113-114.
23 Ibid., p. 213-215.
24 Ibid., pp. 99-106, 280.
25 Ibid., p. 280.

they opposed his directive? Did God reveal an imperfectly contradictory (*nāqiṣī*) religion and ask men to help him in order to perfect it, or is it they who have joined themselves (*shurkā*) to God?;"[26] "They [the *mujtahids*] bring the Western way of life and they no longer have any confidence in Islam, in God and in the Prophet."[27] For Abū al-Qāsim Khān, the fact that the *mujtahid*s justify the possibility that they might contradict each other on some points of the law demonstrates, in itself, that they recognize the impossibility of attaining truth through *ijtihād*: "Every *mujtahid* who, using *ijtihād*, issues fatwas that run counter to the opinions of his peers is justified (*muṣīb*) because they themselves do not claim that it is possible through the use of *ijtihād* to establish the truth on any subject whatsoever."[28]

In the last part of the work, however, Abū al-Qāsim Khān proposes, in essence, to give back to the terms *ijtihād*, *mujtahid*, *taqlīd*, and *muqallid* the meaning that, in his opinion, they should have in the eyes of Muslims: "If the aim of *ijtihād* is to attempt to know and understand the principles and the derivations of those principles that define a thing as permitted or forbidden, then we must all be *mujtahid*s. In that case, we are all *muqallid*s of the Imams who are the representatives who have been authorized to express themselves in the name of God."[29]

Moreover, he insists on this concept at length in the conclusion of his work:

> In conclusion, and to summarize, we can state that the doctrine of *ijtihād* and of *taqlīd*, which consists of dividing men into two categories, the *mujtahid*s and the *muqallids*, in the sense that most people give to these words, is invalid (*ṣaḥīḥ nīst*) in Shi'i theology. ... But if these two words take the meaning that they may have had in the *akhbār* [that is to say the *taqlīd* following the infallibles Imams], a meaning which is in general not given to them at all and which does not result in the said theories [those of the *uṣūlī*s], then these words can be used. ... This *taqlīd* commanded by the Imams must not be carried out exclusively by the ignorant but also by the ulemas. The ulemas must exercise their *taqlīd* from the Imām as well as consulting and using the *akhbār*s passed on by a trustworthy man. ... Thus, according to this principle, *taqlīd* following anyone else but the Imām makes no sense. It is, then, possible for us to use the word *mujtahid* to designate the entire community and all Shi'as if by that we mean exerting oneself to understand the rulings of the Imām (*ḥukm-i Imām*) and to respect them.[30]

Thus, in rehabilitating the words *mujtahid* and *ijtihād*, Abū al-Qāsim Khān proposes a unique argumentation that is distinguishable in several ways from that of the *akhbārī* ulemas. Muḥammad Amīn al-Astarābādī's main focus was on trying to demonstrate that this division between *muqallid*s and *mujtahid*s had its origin in Sunnism: "This division (*taqsīm*), that is, the division of the populace into *mujtahid*s and *muqallid*s, and [the application of] its related stipulations and rules have occurred in imitation of the Sunni jurisprudents, inasmuch as they divided the

26 Ibid., p. 25.
27 Ibid., p. 112.
28 Ibid., p. 31.
29 Ibid., p. 234.
30 Ibid., pp. 247-248.

people after the prophet into two groups, *mujtahid*s and *muqallid*s. ... The truth is that these premises hold only for those who do not confess the necessity of adherence to the Chaste Descendants [i.e., the Twelver Shiite Imams] and do not render them a means toward the understanding on the Book of God and the Sunnah of His Prophet. An Imami could only hold such an opinion out of ignorance of this important point."[31] And yet, the argumentation of Abū al-Qāsim Khān does meet in that Al-Astarābādī explained that certainties were the source of serenity and peace whereas conjectures only bring disturbance: "Reason and revelation both demonstrate that the benefit of sending prophets and revealing scripture is to remove disagreement and disputes among the believers so that their lives in this world and the next might be in order. But if speculation is considered a permissible method of interpretation with regard to God's rules of law, then this benefit is lost through the occurrence of disagreement and disputes, as is plainly observable."[32]

C. The Origins of ijtihād *and Its Development in the Shi'i Context*

A large part of the beginning of *Ijtihād wa taqlīd* consists of returning to the origins of *ijtihād* within Shi'ism and explaining to the reader how what Abū al-Qāsim Khān considers a historical drama came about. He sees it as primarily the result of a progressive imitation of Sunni legal methods. He insists, therefore, on the importance of Abū Ḥanīfa to this process, but has almost nothing to say about the particular Shi'i scholars, not even mentioning al-'Allāma al-Ḥillī (d. 726/1325), who was one of the most important representatives of the so-called Hillah school and who in fact theorized the division of the community into the two categories of *mujtahid*s on the one hand and *muqallid*s on the other.[33] Abū al-Qāsim Khān does, however, very briefly refer to Muḥammad b. Idris Ḥillī (d. 598/1201), whose work *al-Sarā'ir* had a great impact and who presented *ijtihād* as one of the bases of law.[34] Abū al-Qāsim Khān also attributes this great interest in *'aql* (reason) in legal scholarship to a faulty interpretation of the works translated from Greek in the eighth, ninth, and tenth centuries, especially under the caliphates of Hārūn al-Rashīd (d. 193/809) and al-Mā'mūn (d. 217/833). The fact that the development of logic (*manṭiq*) and of *kalām* in the Middle Ages was essentially the work of Sunni scholars is evidence, in Abū al-Qāsim Khān's eyes, that *ijtihād* and Usulism do in fact both have their origins in Sunnism.[35] These

31 Quoted by Stewart in *Islamic Legal Orthodoxy*, p. 193.

32 Quoted by Stewart in *Islamic Legal Orthodoxy*, p. 186.

33 On the school of Hillah and on al-'Allāma al-Ḥillī in particular, see Sabine Schmidtke, *The Theology of al- 'Allama al-Hilli (d. 726/1325)*, Berlin: Klaus Schwarz Verlag, 1991.

34 Abū al-Qāsim Khān Ibrāhīmī, *Ijtihād wa taqlīd*, pp. 58-59.

35 Ibid., p. 231.

Sunni and Greek origins of *ijtihād* within Shi'ism were also pointed out by many *akhbārī* ulemas.[36]

And yet, although Abū al-Qāsim Khān calls this evolution "ugly" (*zisht*),[37] comparing it to polluted water that prevents a flower (here, Islam) from growing and flourishing,[38] he also plays down the consequences of this evolution, emphasizing that there have always been Shi'as who refused this belief and these evolutions.[39]

Abū al-Qāsim Khān starts with several preliminaries that he puts forward so that the reader will be able to understand his argumentation. To begin with, neither *ijtihād* nor the science of the principles (*'ilm-i uṣūl*) existed, according to him, during the Prophet's lifetime.[40] It was inconceivable then for Muslims to issue rulings independently of the Prophet. Every decision was taken after having asked Muḥammad, and he was the only one who could determine limits (*ḥadd*) in legal matters, so he had to be asked. *Ijtihād* emerged during the development of the science of principles (*'ilm-i uṣūl*), which Abū al-Qāsim Khān explicitly condemns:

> They considered the understanding of the book and of the *ḥadīth* to pass through this science.[41]
> It is starting at that moment that the personal opinion of the *mujtahid*, acquired thanks to this science, became [similar to] God's ruling and that it became compulsory for the *muqallid* to submit to it and to recognize it as a ruling from God and from the Prophet. So they divided the community of the Prophet into two categories, the *mujtahids* and the *muqallids* of the *mujtahids* (the imitators of the *mujtahids*).[42]
> This science, along with *ijtihād*, became for the *mujtahid* the book of God and the tradition of the Prophet.[43]

According to Abū al-Qāsim Khān, when the Prophet, in the oasis of *ghadīr khumm*, declared *ḥalāl* to be *ḥalāl* (the allowed to be allowed) and *ḥarām* to be *ḥarām* (the forbidden to be forbidden) until the rise (*qiyām*) of the Twelfth Imām, he affirmed the impossibility, in effect, of resorting to *ijtihād*, to *qiyās*, or to *rā'y*. Moreover, on that same day, by designating 'Alī as his *walī* and his successor, the Prophet restricted religious authority to his only son-in-law. From then on, the methods employed by those who divided the fledgling Muslim community are similar to *ijtihād*. Thus, Abū Bakr (d. 13/634) is presented as the one who opened the door to *ijtihād* on the death of the Prophet, usurping 'Alī's rights and claiming the status of "successor of the Prophet of God" (*khālīfa rasūl Allāh*). In addition,

36 Stewart, "The Genesis of the Akhbari Revival," p. 169.
37 Abū al-Qāsim Khān Ibrāhīmī, *Ijtihād wa taqlīd*, p. 12.
38 Ibid., p. 99.
39 Ibid., p. 12.
40 Ibid., p. 12.
41 Ibid., p. 10.
42 Ibid.
43 Ibid., p. 9.

Abū al-Qāsim Khān adds that the Prophet never commanded anything that was not asked of him by God:

> What [the Prophet] pronounced came from the spirit of God and not from his own decision or from the air (*havā'ī*), but they [Abū Bakr and his partisans] practiced their own *ijtihād* and issued their own opinions. It is clear that the reasoning (*'aql*) of the people does not make it possible for them to establish the truth but that, on the contrary, it is a source of corruption (*fasād*), such that religious feeling itself disappears and they are left with nothing at all in their hands.[44]
>
> Because they [Abū Bakr and his partisans] no longer relied on the Qur'ān and on answers given by the Prophet, they began to use *ijtihād*.[45]
>
> How is it that the masses can accept these beliefs [the *ijtihād* of the *mujtahids*]? Is it possible to find a religious doctrine that is any weaker than this one? What is the difference between this doctrine and the faith that after the death of the Prophet it is up to the people to decide who is the caliph and who is not? It is obvious that these are practices based on conjectures.[46]

As a result, the recognition of *ijtihād* is connected with the legitimation of the very methods that Abū Bakr used against 'Alī. Abū al-Qāsim Khān indicates that beyond the *fitna* (division) created by Abū Bakr and 'Umar (d. 23/644) in order to seize power on the death of the Prophet by resorting to *ijtihād* to argue against the rights that had been accorded to 'Alī by the Prophet, Abū Bakr and 'Umar also resorted to *ijtihād* to intervene on all sorts of subjects about which they knew nothing.[47] *Ijtihād* is therefore explicitly associated with the earliest practices of the enemies of 'Alī and with a kind of ruse, by the Qurayshites who converted to Islam belatedly, in order to free themselves from the prophecy of Muḥammad and from Islam. Abū al-Qāsim Khān also associates *ijtihād* with blameworthy (*bid'at*) innovations.[48] Likewise, the arguments used by Mu'awiyya (d. 60/680) to set off the war against 'Alī, notably at Ṣiffīn in 37/657, are also compared to *ijtihād*: "It is known that the rejection of religion and of authority provoked a large number of disturbances, conflicts, wars, and massacres. All of the disturbances that have been seen in Islam have their origins in this approach. Moreover, it was said that Mu'awiyya was a *mujtahid* and that in his *ijtihād* he referred to the war against 'Alī as a necessary (*lāzim*) one."[49] This reasoning, consisting of associating certain legal methods, such as *ijtihād* or *ijmā'*, with the practices of the enemies of Imām 'Alī, was also taken up by some of the *akhbārī* ulemas. So, for instance, Muḥsin Fayḍ al-Kāshānī (d. 1091/1680) said that *ijmā'* was invented by Abū Bakr.

---

44 Ibid., p. 16.
45 Ibid.
46 Ibid., p. 144.
47 Ibid., p. 17.
48 Ibid., p. 48.
49 Ibid., p. 168.

According to Abū al-Qāsim Khān, new Sufi institutions, such as the *khānaqāh*, the *zāwiyā*, and the *ribāṭ*, none of which he considers legitimate in any way, were also established in the name of *ijtihād*.[50]

The Reasons for the Shift towards ijtihād *within Shi'ism*

Abū al-Qāsim Khān presents the founders of *ijtihād* within Shi'ism as fundamentally power-hungry men who were envious of the ways in which Sunni legal scholars could use *ijtihād*, whether in the form of analogical reasoning (*qiyās*) or of personal opinion (*rā'y*).[51] Some even tried, he says, to obtain the authorization to exercise the *ijtihād* (*ijāza-yi ijtihād*) of the historical Imams, but without success. But at the time of the Occultation they tried again to claim the practice of *ijtihād*. According to Abū al-Qāsim Khān, the "*uṣūlī* clerics did not understand that they were transforming Shi'i *fiqh* into the same *fiqh* that the opponents of Shi'ism had established, and that their methods were becoming like those of the Sunnis."[52] In addition, Abū al-Qāsim Khān reminds his readers on several occasions that the Sunni religious scholars who initiated this process, such as Abū Ḥanīfa, were opponents of the Imams. Abū Ḥanīfa in fact went as far as to systematically issue fatwas that contradicted the rulings of the Imām: "One of their fundamental principles was to oppose the Imams, and it had become the rule for Abū Ḥanīfa to use *ijtihād* for every subject that remained unclear. He asked what the legal advice of the Imām [Ja'far Ṣādiq] was on the given subject and then issued a fatwa that was its exact opposite."[53] Incidentally, Abū al-Qāsim Khān cursed Abū Ḥanīfa in this treatise.[54] He says that in Sunnism, the requirement to choose a *mujtahid* had become so important that their ulemas declared that the prayers of anyone who did not have a *mujtahid* would be invalid (*bāṭil*): "They declared that he who is neither *mujtahid* nor *muqallid* will find his prayer invalid because it is not possible to come nearer to God while remaining ignorant. Therefore, they have made the *mujtahids* into the equals of the Imams. They even called their religious scholars 'Imām', like Imām Abū Ḥanīfa and Imām Shāfi'ī."[55]

Although the lack of any obvious foundation within Shi'i Islam for *ijtihād* and for the recourse to *'aql* in order to authenticate *ḥadīths* causes Abū al-Qāsim Khān to think that this *uṣūlī* conviction was essentially a way for the clergy to seize some of the functions of the Prophet and of the Imams, such as tax collection or the leading of prayers, we should also note that he writes several times that he

---

50 Ibid., p. 20. On the refutation of Sufism within Shaykhi doctrine, see Hermann, *Le shaykhisme à la période qajare. Histoire sociale et doctrinale d'une École chiite*.

51 Abū al-Qāsim Khān Ibrāhīmī, *Ijtihād wa taqlīd*, p. 35.

52 Ibid., p. 60.

53 Ibid., p. 49.

54 Ibid., p. 37.

55 Ibid., p. 49.

understands the attraction of *ijtihād* among the Shi'as, saying that the ulemas who justified the use of *ijtihād* felt confused at the beginning of the Occultation, a period known as the period of "perplexity" (*ḥayra*), and perceived *ijtihād* as a solution.[56] In this context, Abū al-Qāsim Khān brings up Shaykh Tūsī (d. 460/1067), who introduced *ijtihād* into Shi'ism, in particular in his work *Mabsūṭ*, in what he describes as a very difficult time for the Shi'i community.[57] He also mentions two Shi'i scholars who, in his opinion, played an important role in the development of *ijtihād*, Ḥasan b. Abī 'Aqīl 'Umānī and Muḥammad b. Janīd Iskānī. These two contributed to the enrichment of Shi'i libraries with books on *ijtihād*.[58]

Thus, Abū al-Qāsim Khān also presents the *mujtahid*s as people who are unable to "endure" the wait for the Imām of the Time.[59] According to him, the substance of the *mujtahid*'s thinking is as follows: "Because the door to religious studies (*'ilm*) is closed (*masdūd*) but our obligation is nevertheless to respect the religious rulings, it is necessary to resort to *ijtihād*, that is to use our own belief (*gumān*) to issue religious rulings."[60] Gradually, the majority of Shi'i believers became *muqallid*s, in a position like that of the Sunnis, forced to choose their *marja'*s or their *mujtahids* from among four dead legal scholars: Abū Ḥanīfa, Mālik ibn Anas (d. 179/795), Shāfi'ī (d. 206/821-822), and Ibn Ḥanbal (d. 241/855).[61] Thus, Abū al-Qāsim Khān sorrowfully evokes these Shi'as, a people without knowledge who consider everything that the *mujtahid*s report in their fatwas as "established" (*yaqīn*) and therefore refuse to see the commands of the Prophet and the Imams as genuine.[62] This belief, which creates disturbances (*fasād*), is in fact inspired in the *mujtahid* by the devil (*shayṭān*) himself and becomes a kind of assistance for him: "Why do you [the *mujtahid*] have to help the devil? ... If your goal was to reform religion, then you should know that that is the role of the [Hidden] Imām."[63] Muḥammad Amīn al-Astarābādī also evoked this division between the *mujtahid*s and the *muqallid*s, using the word *ḥaṣr* (containment, restriction) to point out the monopoly on religious authority that the *mujtahid*s tried to seize for themselves. Thus, he speaks of the "restriction of the people" (*ḥaṣr al-ra'īyah fī al-mujtahid wa'l-muqallid*).[64]

We have already emphasized that Abū al-Qāsim Khān nevertheless considered that there had always been Shi'i scholars, in every period, who were opposed to this evolution of *fiqh* and to the use of *ijtihād*. However, we note that when he men-

56 Ibid.
57 Ibid., pp. 51, 54.
58 Ibid., pp. 56-58.
59 Ibid., p. 142.
60 Ibid., p. 78.
61 Ibid., p. 21.
62 Ibid., p. 88.
63 Ibid., p. 162.
64 Stewart, *Islamic Legal Orthodoxy*, p. 192, footnote 61.

tioned these scholars, he did not explicitly name *akhbārī* scholars. But while Abū al-Qāsim Khān did ascribe several faults to the *akhbārīs*, he in no way compared them to the *uṣūlīs*. According to Abū al-Qāsim Khān, while the *akhbārīs* fought against *ijtihād* and explicitly distanced themselves from it, they also sometimes made errors in their practice and resorted to conjectures (*ẓann*), possibly unconsciously: "Even if the claims of the *akhbārīs* are correct when they declare that the use of conjectures is forbidden (*ḥarām*); that this revolution by means of which the ulemas used the Qur'ān, the tradition of the Prophet, and consensus on the basis of rational decisions is unauthorized; and that the scholarship of the legal establishment of ruling must be acquired by revelation; they [the *akhbārī* scholars] nevertheless acted differently. Their argumentation remains insufficient and they did not manage to make clear how they acquired their scholarship. They themselves, in reality, relied on conjectures. Some of their arguments, in addition, are explicitly conjectural. They fell into the same trap as did the *uṣūlīs*."[65] Abū al-Qāsim Khān also calls the methodology employed by the *akhbārīs* "a form of simplicity" (*nū'-i sādigī*).[66] But as we shall see, it is essentially because of their lack of knowledge of the doctrine of the *rukn-i rābi'* that Abū al-Qāsim Khān judges that the *akhbārīs* are not any more successful at proposing a doctrine that will bring serenity to the believer and allow him to have a faith that rests on certainties. And yet, as we have already seen, he does not see the *uṣūlī* and *akhbārī* ulemas as equals, affirming that "the method of the *uṣūlīs* is a thousand times weaker than that of the *akhbārīs*."[67]

According to Abū al-Qāsim Khān, the vehemence of the Sunni ulemas against Shi'ism, along with the important political and social role played by the proponents of *ijtihād* within Shi'ism, therefore forced the Shi'i ulemas who were faithful to the cause of the Imams to practice an "extremely rigorous *taqiyya*" (*taqiyya-yi shadīda*).[68] In this context he evokes the fear in which Ibn Babūya lived because of the repression of Shi'ism but also explains that, fortunately, the men who are "proofs" (*ḥujjat*) of God have patience.[69] And yet, Abū al-Qāsim Khān notes that the situation is now different and that Shi'as certainly have more opportunities to express themselves. Therefore, the predominance of Usulism among the Shi'as is no longer tolerable: "Today, thanks be to God, we are not afraid of the Sunnis and are no longer forced into such a strict *taqiyya* towards them. From now on scholars can enjoy a certain liberty and can better express their opinions."[70]

---

65 Abū al-Qāsim Khān Ibrāhīmī, *Ijtihād wa taqlīd*, pp. 60-61.
66 Ibid., p. 127.
67 Ibid.
68 Ibid., p. 213.
69 Ibid., p. 275.
70 Ibid.

There are many ways in which the reasoning of Abū al-Qāsim Khān agrees with that of *akhbārī* ulemas of the Safavid period, ulemas as influential as Muḥammad Amīn al-Astarābādī, al-Ḥurr al-ʿĀmilī, and Muḥsin Fayḍ al-Kāshānī, but there are also some occasionally very important distinctions. While Abū al-Qāsim Khān's arguments appear to be sound, we do need to note that he never entered into the details of the history of the *uṣūlī* scholars and texts. This may have been a matter of avoiding the mention of particular figures and making it easier for the ordinary Shiʿa, who was not erudite in *fiqh*, to understand his treatise. As Devin Stewart has pointed out, the *akhbārī* scholars, for their part, acted like veritable "historians of Islamic Law and the Twelver Madhhab,"[71] wanting to alert their coreligionists to the jeopardin in which *uṣūlī* legal methods placed Shi'ism. Thus, Muḥammad Amīn al-Astarābādī was addressing the *fuqahā*. But we could also imagine that it was more prudent for Abū al-Qāsim Khān not to explicitly name the most important *fuqahā* of the history of Usulism. In his analysis of *al-Fawā'id al-madaniyya*, Devin Stewart points out in particular that Muḥammad Amīn al-Astarābādī only indirectly criticized his contemporary al-Shahīd al-Thānī, although he may well have been the person most directly targeted in that work.[72] Shahīd al-Thānī obtained the status of *mujtahid* just after his return, in 944/1537-38, from Cairo, where he had studied Shafiʿī law, and he played a central role in the increasingly important reliance on reason as the basis for establishing Shiʿi law.[73] Al-Astarābādī was of course conscious of the danger that he was running and referred to it explicitly in his work: "It became necessary that I reveal this, and no one's censure prevented me from fulfilling my obligation to God. So I have revealed it, and God will protect me from the people."[74]

The *akhbārī* ulemas pointed out very precise lines of kinship between the most influential *uṣūlī* legal texts and Sunni legal literature, which Abū al-Qāsim Khān did not do. According to Muḥammad Amīn al-Astarābādī, the first Shiʿi legal scholar who explicitly used Sunni legal methods was Muḥammad b. Aḥmad b. al-Junayd (d. 298/910), who adopted *qiyās*. Shaykh Mufid (d. 413/1022) took inspiration from that, and his students al-Sharīf al-Murtaḍā (d. 436/1044) and Shaykh al-Ṭūsī (d. 460/1067) adopted other Sunni legal methods over the course of the eleventh century. Then al-ʿAllāmah al-Ḥillī pushed the process further, and was in turn imitated by al-Shahīd al-Awwal during the fourteenth century, then ʿAlī b. ʿAbd al-ʿAlī al-Karakī and al-Shahīd al-Thānī, in the sixteenth century.[75] In this context, we can also refer to this passage from *al-Fawā'id al-madaniyya*: "It has be-

71 Stewart, *Islamic Legal Orthodoxy*, p. 202.
72 Stewart, "The Genesis of the Akhbari Revival," p. 173.
73 Stewart, *Islamic Legal Orthodoxy*, pp. 204-205.
74 Ibid., p. 194.
75 Ibid., pp. 193-194, 203-204.

come well known among the scholars that the *Tahdhīb* of al-'Allāmah al-Ḥillī is an abridgment of the *Mukhtaṣar* of Ibn al-Ḥājib, which is an abridgment of the *Muntahā* of Ibn al-Ḥājib, which is an abridgment of the *Iḥkām* of al-Āmidī, which is an abridgment of the *Maḥṣūl* of Fakhr al-Dīn al-Rāzī, which is an abridgment of the *Mu'tamad* of Abū 'l-Ḥusayn al-Baṣrī."[76] Other *akhbārī* ulemas invoked this development. Al-Kāshānī also pointed out these relationships between Sunni and Shi'i legal scholars in the medieval period, which resulted, in his opinion, in the importation of Sunni legal methods into Shi'i law: "When the epoch of the infallible Imams came to an end and the intermediaries (*sufarā'*) between them and their supporters (*shī'atihim*) had been cut off, their absence became difficult to endure and the reign of the usurpers had gone on for a long time. The Shiites mixed with the Sunnis and became familiar with their books as youths, since they were the books commonly taught in the colleges, mosques, and elsewhere – for the kings and government officials were Sunnis, and subjects always follow the lead of their kings and government officials. The Shiites studied the religious sciences together with the Sunnis and read the *uṣūl-i fiqh* works which the Sunnis had written in their aim to facilitate the speculation upon which their legal rulings were based. They approved of some of what the Sunnis had written and disapproved of some. This led them to write books on this science, either corroborating it or detracting from it. They discussed matters which neither the Prophet nor the infallible Imams had brought forth, but which the Sunnis had discussed. They increased the number of questions concerning these topics and confounded the jurists with regard to the methods of legal proof."[77] And again, "When the works of our fellows on [*ijmā'* and *ijtihād*] increased in number, and they discussed *uṣūl al-fiqh* and its branches using the Sunnis' terminology, the juridical methodology and terminology of the two sects (*ṭā'ifatān*) came to resemble one another. This brought about the effect that some [Shi'ite legal scholars] became thoroughly confused, to such an extent that they claimed it was permissible to perform *ijtihād*, give legal rulings on the basis of personal opinion, set down rules and stipulations for such matters, and interpret ambiguous passages [in the sacred texts] through conjecture, estimation, and the adoption of opinions merely because they are widely accepted (*al-akhdh bi-'ttifāqi 'l-ārā'*)."[78] Al-Ḥurr al-'Āmilī, for his part, said that the Shi'i legal scholars continued to admire Sunni legal treatises and even considered it to be a religious obligation (*farḍ-i kifāya*) for them to be versed in Sunni legal literature,[79] even while al-Ḥurr al-'Āmilī himself personally

76 Quoted and translated by Stewart, Ibid., p. 191.

77 Al-Kāshānī, *Safinat al-najāt*, pp. 9-10, quoted and translated by Stewart, *Islamic Legal Orthodoxy*, pp. 197-198.

78 Al-Kāshānī, *Safinat al-najāt*, p. 11, quoted and translated by Stewart, *Islamic Legal Orthodoxy*, p. 198.

79 Al-Ḥurr al-'Āmilī, *al-Fawā'id al-ṭūsiyya*, p. 252, and mentioned by Stewart, *Islamic Legal Orthodoxy*, p. 200.

considered this usage to be "diabolical:" "the evils of studying their works are many and obvious; the least of them is approval of them concerning points that are not known to be in agreement with the Imams or are in contradiction to them."[80] This line of argumentation by the *akhbārī* scholars about the kinship between Sunni and *uṣūlī* legal methods, developed in particular by al-'Allāmah al-Ḥillī, seemed particularly pertinent to several researchers, including Devin Stewart and Ahmad Kazemi Moussavi.[81] Devin Stewart also pointed out that some Sunni treatises, such as the Malekite legal scholar Ibn al-Ḥājib (d. thirteenth century)'s *Mukhtaṣar* and the commentary on that work by the Shafi'ī legal scholar 'Aḍud al-Dīn 'Abd al-Raḥmān al-Ījī (d. 756/1355), entitled *al-Sharḥ al-'Aḍudī*, became indispensable parts of the curriculum for Shi'i legal study.[82]

The reasoning used by Abū al-Qāsim Khān in which he associated certain legal methods, such as *ijtihād*, with the practices of the enemies of Imām 'Alī was also used by some *akhbārī* scholars. Thus, al-Kāshānī wrote that *ijmā'* was invented by the Sunnis to justify the caliphate of Abū Bakr.[83]

Like Abū al-Qāsim Khān, al-Astarābādī pointed out that in spite of this evolution in Shi'i law, there was always a handful of ulemas who remained faithful to the teachings of the Imams. Al-Astarābādī was surely thinking of the first scholars who compiled collections of *ḥadīth*s when he called such ulemas the "old Shi'i ulemas" (*qudamā' aṣḥābinā*) in distinction to the "later Shi'i ulemas" (*jam' min muta'akhkhirī aṣḥābinā*) who adopted Sunni legal methods.[84] In the medieval period, these proto-*akhbārī*s were also called *aṣḥāb al-ḥadīth* (companions of the *ḥadīth*)[85] or designated by the pejorative term *ḥashiwiyya* (low-level scholars).[86] But the explanation by the *akhbārī* scholars of the Safavid period that involved identifying authors of the Buyid period such as Shaykh Mufid, al-Sharīf al-Murtaḍā, and Shaykh al-Ṭūsī as proto-*akhbārī*s appears dubious to D. Stewart, because these Buyid-period scholars called themselves *fuqahā* or *uṣūlīyūn* and were openly opposed to the term *aṣḥāb al-ḥadīth*. In addition, the Buyid-era scholars supported the authority of legal specialists over that of *ḥadīth* specialists.[87]

For Abū al-Qāsim Khān and his predecessors, nevertheless, it does not seem as though this evolution in Shi'i law can be explained primarily by the gradual in-

---

80 Quoted and translated by Stewart in "The Genesis of the Akhbari Revival," pp. 184-185.

81 See Ahmad Kazemi Moussavi, *Religious Authority in Shi'ite Islam. From the Office of Mufti to the Institution of Marja'*, Kuala Lumpur: International Institute of Islamic Thoughts and Civilization, 1996, pp. 26, 30, 85, 170.

82 Stewart, *Islamic Legal Orthodoxy*, p. 97.

83 Ibid., p. 188.

84 Ibid., p. 56.

85 Ibid., p. 182.

86 Newman, "The Development and Political Significance of the Rationalist (*Uṣūlī*) and Traditionalist (*Akhbārī*) Schools in Imāmī Shī'ī History From the Third/Ninth to the Tenth/Sixteen Century A.D." (Ph.D. dissertation, UCLA, Los Angeles, 1986), p. 56.

87 Stewart, *Islamic Legal Orthodoxy*, p. 206.

fluence of Sunni law on Shi'i legal experts. The thirst for power, whether political, social, or economic, played an absolutely central role in this process. This evolution within the mainstream of Shi'ism, then, is part of the inevitable domination by the forces of ignorance in this world. This interpretation was also developed by the *akhbārī* ulemas of the Safavid period, especially Ibrāhīm al-Qaṭīfī (d. after 945/1539-40),[88] although perhaps not on the same scale as in Kirmānī Shaykhism. One other historical factor, however, was not mentioned either by Abū al-Qāsim Khān and the Shaykhī masters or by most of the Safavid era *akhbārī* ulemas, and that is the role of the Shi'i regimes and of their religious policy, particularly of the Buyids and the Safavid states, in this evolution of Shi'i law.[89] It is easy to understand the reasons behind this silence, which was nonetheless broken by some Shi'i ulemas who lived in the Arab world or Iran during the Safavid and Zand era. For ulemas living in Iran during the sixteenth and seventeenth centuries, such a mention of the Safavid could have been understand on the one hand as a critique of the state, but also, on the other hand, as a critique of the process of Shi'itization of the Iranian plateau. Therefore, this question became an inarguably existential one for the Shi'as of Iran starting in the Safavid era, and one that was also difficult to bring up for the Shi'as outside Iran, who often perceived Iran as the heart of the Shi'i world and as an indispensable exterior support.

D. Fiqh, *Islam, and Reason* ('aql)

This reasoning of Abū al-Qāsim Khān's against *ijtihād* connects very naturally with a certain kind of rhetoric about the meaning of reason (*'aql*) in Islam and in *fiqh*. Abū al-Qāsim Khān writes several times that more than 70 Qur'anic verses and more than 1200 *ḥadīth*s completely leave out any use of *ẓann* and therefore of *qiyās*, of *rā'y*, or of *ijtihād* as well as of any rationalist argument that is independent on revelation, especially in legal matters.[90] He returns to this basic concept many times:

> There is no need to resort to *ijtihād*. ... If people are today the servants of God and are devoted (*'abūdīyat*) to him, why do they need to attach themselves to the *mujtahid* with all the problems that he creates in their religion? If we believe that our duty (*dhama*) is to be devoted to God and to his Prophet and that the rulings of the Prophet and of the Imams have been passed on to us, that is sufficient and rightful. ... Therefore, why do we need *ijtihād*? If there are some who claim that the *ijtihād* of the *mujtahid* solves our problems, we ask them to justify this right. Can they show us even one single Qur'anic verse and one single *akhbār*? As for us, we have 70 Qur'anic verses and 1200 *ḥadīth*s that refute their argumentation.[91]

---

88 Newman, "The Development and Political Significance," pp. 777, 783, 795-796.

89 This issue was also brought up by Stewart, *Islamic Legal Orthodoxy*, p. 198.

90 Abū al-Qāsim Khān Ibrāhīmī, *Ijtihād wa taqlīd*, pp. 26-27, 65.

91 Ibid., p. 95.

Abū al-Qāsim Khān tries to show, using several precise examples, that the law is immutable and that the use of reason (*'aql*) does not allow us to grasp all of the subtleties. A number of times, he uses the example of the number of cycles (*rakat*) that is required in canonical prayer. Thus, no-one can establish, using reason, why it is required to perform two cycles during the morning prayer (*fajr*), then four for the noon prayer (*ẓuhr*), and three for the evening prayer (*maghrib*). If there is a logical reason for this, then at any rate men do not know it. On the other hand, it is intelligible to the Prophet and the Imams.[92] Men are however capable of understanding the concept of divine unity (*tawḥīd*) thanks to reason, because that is a matter of complete order (*amr-i kullī*).

This principled stance on the impossibility of resorting to reason to establish *fiqh* seems to Abū al-Qāsim Khān to have been justified several times during the life of the Prophet, because he questioned or reconsidered some of his rulings and his opinions were then either confirmed or alternatively overturned by God. Therefore, since the opinion of the infallible Prophet was sometimes corrected by God, it is never acceptable to refer to that of a *mujtahid*.[93]

Abū al-Qāsim Khān then mocks those who think that they can produce an absolute (*qaṭ'ī*) jurisprudence using reason. He also adds that while these *fuqahā* were influenced by the Greek tradition, it nevertheless remains the case that they did not understand how the Greeks saw the use of reason. According to Abū al-Qāsim Khān, resorting to logic (*manṭiq*) only made sense to the Greeks in the context of science (*'ilm*). In no way was this tradition a basis for proposing a *fiqh* resulting from any form of logic and then comparing it to the law revealed to the Prophet:

> In their books dedicated to logic, the Greeks indicated that logic is scientific (*'ilmī*) and that respecting its principles makes it possible to preserve oneself from errors, on the condition, of course, that it is used appropriately. Thus, the use of logic makes it possible to correct possible errors. The importance of thought (*fikr*) based on logic cannot mean that men gifted with logic can replace the Prophet, that they cannot make mistakes, and that they are infallible. They are mistaken when they think that resorting to logic will of itself save them from all possible confusion.[94]

This passage is also interesting because it emphasizes the fact that Abū al-Qāsim Khān does not condemn the Greek sages and scholars per se, but rather the use of their concepts by some Muslim scholars who want to apply them to *fiqh*. This is an important point because it calls into question a particular understanding that was widespread among the *uṣūlī* ulemas and also often shared by the rest of society, namely that the scholars who were devoted to the scriptural sources were indifferent or even hostile to philosophical thought, Western or otherwise, a con-

92 Ibid., pp. 29, 84, 121-122.
93 Ibid., pp. 83-83.
94 Ibid., p. 71.

ception which, furthermore, served to give their practice of Islam the appearance of being backward or maladapted to modernity.

The Reasoning and Science of ḥadīth

In this work, Abū al-Qāsim Khān also returns to the prohibition on resorting to reason in order to critique *ḥadīth* and even to discard some of the *ḥadīths*. In this way, he clearly indicates that in the name of reason the *mujtahid* are not only modifying *sharī'a* by issuing new religious rulings, but also calling into question the corpus of *ḥadīths*, which in his eyes makes up the Shi'as' most valuable possession:

> The cleric who criticizes the *akhbārs* and eliminates some of them has fallen into unbelief (*kufr*) and associationism (*shirk*) and has per se denied God himself. It is forbidden to all Shi'as to reject the traditions of an Imam or to judge an *akhbār* by the standards of reason (*'aql*). In addition, the Imams declared that if you hear of an *akhbār* who proclaims that the day is night and the night is day you are required to accept that. You do not have the right to set that aside, even if you are not required to put it into practice, if it appears to be totally incompatible with other legal traditions. Nevertheless, it remains forbidden to reject it.[95]
>
> If they reject every *akhbārs* that does not agree with their *'aql* there will soon be no more traditions of the Imams, because there are many *mujtahids*. If every one of them refutes an *akhbār*, there will soon no longer be any trace of the tradition of the Prophet.[96]
>
> He who, in spite of everything, rejects some of the *akhbārs* is refusing one of the commandments of God, the Prophet, and the Imams. This is a blasphemous (*kufr*) practice.[97]

To emphasize the extreme importance of guarding the *ḥadīths*, Abū al-Qāsim Khān points out that the first Shi'i works that were written at the end of the era of the historic Imams and the beginning of the Occultation are precisely collections of *ḥadīths*, which indicates very clearly that the Imams did not authorize these ulemas to write whatever they wanted to on the basis of personal reason, and that the ulemas respected the absolute authority of the Imams:

> Look carefully at the most important works of the [Shi'i] ulemas that are still in existence and that are still used by the Shi'as. You will see that there is nothing else in them besides the words of the Imams. It is thanks to these traditions that we can declare that such-and-such a thing is permitted, such-and-such a thing is required, and such-and-such another is forbidden. In these works, there is nothing but what is sufficient (*kāfī ast*)[98].[99]

---

95 Ibid., p. 41.

96 Ibid., p. 42.

97 Ibid., pp. 148-149.

98 This last mention is an obvious allusion to one of the most important collections of *ḥadīths*, Kulaynī's *Kitāb al-Kāfī*, which means "The Book that Contains Everything that is Sufficient."

99 Abū al-Qāsim Khān Ibrāhīmī, *Ijtihād wa taqlīd*, p. 209.

Still with the aim of emphasizing the importance of the *akhbārs*, in great danger from the clerics' exercise of *'aql*, Abū al-Qāsim Khān reports a *ḥadīth* of the Prophet's that says that anyone who memorizes and transmits 40 *ḥadīths* will be preserved and saved at the resurrection.[100] Therefore, the mission of the ulemas is above all to communicate the *ḥadīths* and to introduce the population to them. In this context, Abū al-Qāsim Khān says: "One single *akhbār* obtained from a 'trustworthy man' has more value than all of the gold and silver, taken together, in this world."[101] and again "My goal is to demonstrate that the Shi'as are those who preserve the *akhbārs* of the Imams. The others are merchants looking for a means of subsistence."[102] We should remember here that the Shaykhī masters carried out their religious duties without receiving any salary. The masters of the Shaykhī school, including Abū al-Qāsim Khān, always had a trade or occupation, usually agricultural, which allowed them to take care of their needs.

Thus, Abū al-Qāsim Khān regularly invites his readers to read the *ḥadīths*, in spite of their multiple meanings, and calls for respect for the *muḥaddithīn* who collected them and who were most often *akhbārī* or proto-*akhbārī* ulemas:

> Thus, we invite all brothers who are believers to refer to the *akhbārs* of the Imams.[103]
> O brothers, we therefore ask you to observe *taqlīd* following the *akhbārs* of the Imams who are now like the successors of the creator (*khulafā-yi parvardigār*). Try to understand them and to obey them. If you cannot achieve this, try with greater thoroughness. It is not more difficult to understand a tradition of the Imams than it is to understand an Arabic poem.[104]
> Our *muḥaddithīn* have produced many efforts. By the grace of God, then, we do not have any *akhbārs* that contradict the Qur'ān. And if there are some, there are very few of them.[105]
> How is it that this question about *ijtihād* and *taqlīd*, which did not exist in Shi'ism at the beginning and which has gradually developed in Sunnism, has managed to influence Shi'i doctrine to the point that it has become a dogma? Why must the [Shi'i] people be permanently in wait for a new treatise on legal practice and not be able to rely on the *akhbārs* of the Imams? If the masses need to consult these *akhbār* in Persian, they exist, and if they wish to consult them in Arabic, they are equally available. It is necessary, God willing, that this error gradually disappear and that the truth be continually reaffirmed by these men [the true ulemas] among their brothers.[106]

---

[100] Ibid., p. 217.
[101] Ibid.
[102] Ibid.
[103] Ibid., p. 229.
[104] Ibid., p. 236.
[105] Ibid., p. 238.
[106] Ibid., pp. 256-257.

E. Abū al-Qāsim Khān Ibrāhīmī's Proposals

Which fiqh *to Adopt?*

The *fiqh* proposed by Abū al-Qāsim Khān is more literal and, therefore, based on the reading of the Qur'ān and of the *akhbārs*. However, an *'alim* may issue a fatwa if its argumentation is perfectly consonant with the Qur'ān and the *akhbār*. If an *'alim* can not find any answer within the Qur'ān or the *akhbār* to a legal question that has been posed, he is obliged to abstain from responding:[107]

> We have no problem in principle with the fact of issuing fatwas and we affirm that it is not forbidden to a legal scholar to issue this kind of ruling if it is not the result of his own deduction but rather the consequence of his reliance on the spirit of the traditions (*rūḥ-i akhbār*), which he must understand in an obvious fashion. If it is the result of conjectures and has not been established (*yaqīn*) it is forbidden for the cleric to issue this fatwa.[108]

Furthermore, the *fiqh* that the Shaykhī Kirmānīs propose does not foresee the use of "legal punishments" (*ḥadd-i sharʿī*), which it is not possible for a religious scholar during the Occultation to pronounce, since only an infallible can take on such a responsibility. This position on legal punishments and "commanding right and forbidding wrong" (*al-amr bi al-maʿrūf wa al-nahy ʿan al-munkar*), the doctrine that is at the basis of all of the political mobilizations in Islam, was already laid out by Muḥammad Karīm Khān: "It is more important in the present time for the ulemas to keep away from worldly affairs and to practice asceticism. According to the doctrine of our masters [the Imams], the *mujtahid* cannot apply legal punishments (*ḥudūd*), such as the death sentence, stoning to death, or whipping sinners. Even commanding right and forbidding wrong (*al-amr bi al-maʿrūf wa al-nahy ʿan al-munkar*) is forbidden in most cases, until the appearance of the Imām of the Time. This is our religion and our course of action. We know that some of the *mujtahids* who do apply legal punishments such as death sentence, stoning to death, or whipping sinners are making mistakes. ... In this time, the distinctinve sign of the pious and ascetic scholar is solitude, retreat, and transmitting the light of the Imams through teaching sciences or other methods, and simply avoiding people."[109]

The "Trustworthy men" (shakhṣ-i thiqa)

The identity of this religious scholar who is able to issue fatwas and, therefore, to introduce the Shiʿas into the occult and non-occult hierarchy of the *rukn-i rābiʿ* is, of course, discussed by Abū al-Qāsim Khān. As a result, he returns in the course

[107] Ibid., pp. 87-90, 206.
[108] Ibid., p. 206.
[109] Muḥammad Karīm Khān, *Sī faṣl*, pp. 37-39.

of his treatise to a fundamental concept, that of the "trustworthy men," who is a "proof" (*ḥujjat*).[110] It is from this person that one can obtain all kinds of information about Islam, particularly in matters of *fiqh*, because this person must be initiated into the *akhbārs*.[111] We have seen that this category of the *rukn-i rābi'* is the equivalent of the true ulemas. A reading of the Shaykhī Kirmānī literature shows that it is this category to which the Shaykhī Kirmānī masters, and therefore also Abū al-Qāsim Khān himself, consider themselves to belong. Muḥammad Khān was possibly one of the Shaykhī masters who was the clearest on this subject, in his *Isḥaqiyya*, completed in 1295/1878-79.[112] In this work, the true ulemas exist to compose "apparent proofs" (*ḥujjat-i ẓāhir*) of God.[113] The Shaykhī Kirmānī masters, then, make up one category of the *rukn-i rābi'*, that of the ulemas, which is below the occult strata. Muḥammad Khān defines them as making up a category that is internal to the Shaykhīs, the category of those who are actively seeking religious knowledge (*'ilm*) and have achieved it.[114] He also describes them as the "results" (*āthār*) of the *nujabā*.[115] There does not seem to be any doubt, by the way, that the Kirmānī disciples, for their part, accord them this status of true ulemas and consider them, therefore, as "proofs" (*ḥujjat*) of God on earth.[116] If that were not the case, they would not have any legitimacy. The masters of the Shaykhī school are therefore associated with one of the categories of the *rukn-i rābi'*, the one that is in a position to initiate believers into knowledge of the *nujabā*.[117] This is probably the meaning they have in mind when, in their works, they invite every Shi'a to seek out the religious scholars who will be able to initiate them into the knowledge of the *nujabā*, which is an obligation inherent to the Occultation in their eyes.

Fearing perhaps that he too will be accused of wanting his disciples to be slavishly devoted, Abū al-Qāsim Khān immediately makes a distinction between the respect that one must have for these "trustworthy men" and the relationship that the *muqallid* maintains with his *mujtahid*.[118] In this way, he makes it clear that the believer who is looking to obtain knowledge from another individual is not necessarily making himself into that person's *muqallid*.

In this way, Abū al-Qāsim Khān regularly reminds his reader that every believer is thus called to look for a "trustworthy man" rather than relying on his

---

110 Abū al-Qāsim Khān, *Ijtihād wa taqlīd*, p. 196.

111 Ibid., pp. 137-139, 142, 147-150.

112 Muḥammad Khān, *Isḥaqiyya*, Kerman: Sa'ādat, 1378/1958-59, pp. 165-166; Muḥammad Karīm Khān, *Sī faṣl*, pp. 31-33.

113 Muḥammad Khān, *Isḥaqiyya*, p. 167.

114 Ibid., pp. 169-170.

115 Ibid., pp. 196-197.

116 Abū al-Qāsim Khān Ibrāhīmī, *Fihrist-i kutub*, p. 22.

117 See the passage dedicated to the ulemas of the third rank in the important work by 'Abd al-Riḍā Khān Ibrāhīmī, *Dūstī-yī dūstān*, particularly pp. 183-187.

118 Abū al-Qāsim Khān Ibrāhīmī, *Ijtihād wa taqlīd*, p. 141.

own reason and thereby becoming lost in conjectures.[119] This is an imperative that is required by the Imams: "The Imams commanded that one should orient oneself towards these trustworthy men. They have enjoined us not to reject these trustworthy men. He who refuses their rulings is like an unbeliever (*kāffir*)."[120] In addition, Abū al-Qāsim Khān quotes many *ḥadīth*s by the third Imām on the fact that the believer should only consult a trustworthy scholar while at the same time pointing out, on several occasions, that very few possess the required characteristics.[121] Not to believe in such an ulema would then be the same as not recognizing the authority of the Imām of the Time himself.[122] These trustworthy men also make it possible for the hearts of believers to be comforted during the Occultation: "When there is a difficulty, it is also true that God has planned a solution, that he will provide it, and that the devout (*ahl-i dīyānat*) can rely on it."[123] In order to emphasize that these trustworthy men are the pure expression of the influence of the Hidden Imām on this world, Abū al-Qāsim Khān also cites *ḥadīth*s on the fact that the hand and the eyes of the Imām remain active forever.[124]

The Necessity of the Nāṭiq-i wāḥid

The work ends with an appendix on the figure of the *nāṭiq-i wāḥid*, which makes up the highest level of the occult hierarchy of the *rukn-i rābi'*. This presentation is consistent with Abū al-Qāsim Khān's arguments about the trustworthy men, because it is the *nāṭiq-i wāḥid* who is the intermediary between the Imām of the Time, on the one hand, and the *nuqabā*, *nujabā*, and *ḥujjat* on the other. Thus, "trustworthy men" are indirectly guided by the *nāṭiq-i wāḥid*. It is only through an acceptance and an understanding of the hidden and apparent elite that the Shi'a can have a comforted heart and absolute confidence in his religion, particularly during the Occultation. For this reason, Abū al-Qāsim Khān refers to the teachings of the Eleventh Imām, who said in his *tafsīr* that the age of the Shi'as of the Imām is approaching.[125]

It is definitely this last point, about the authority given by the doctrine of the *rukn-i rābi'*, that most clearly distinguishes the positions of the *akhbārī* ulemas from those of the Shaykhī Kirmānī masters. If their understanding of the origin and illegitimacy of *ijtihād*, their condemnation of the division of the Shi'i community into two groups (the *mujtahid*s on one side and the *muqallid*s on the other), and their

---

119 Ibid., pp. 158-162, 170-171.
120 Ibid., p. 169.
121 Ibid., pp. 173-174.
122 Ibid., p. 250.
123 Ibid.
124 Ibid., p. 259.
125 Ibid., pp. 278-279. Abū al-Qāsim Khān is referring here to an exegisis of the Qur'ān attributed to the 11th Imām by the Shi'as and known as *Tafsīr al-'Askarī*.

criticism of the monopoly wielded by the *mujtahid*s over religious authority is relatively similar, the solutions they propose diverge in several ways. For the *akhbārī*s, it is essentially the specialists in *ḥadīth*s, namely the *muḥaddithīn*, who have authority, and not the *fuqahā* or the *mujtahid*s.[126] Scholars such as al-Kāshānī, for example, even presented the collections of *ḥadīth*s as guides for believers during the Occultation, which implies a relatively minor role for the ulemas, even the *akhbārī*s and *muḥaddithīn*.[127] In Shaykhism, on the other hand, the true ulema or the "trustworthy man" is a central character, even if his authority is based (mainly) on a thorough knowledge of *ḥadīth*. This figure transmits and explains the traditions of the Imams to believers, but also acts as a link between the Imām of the Time and his occult hierarchy, on the one hand, and the community of believers on the other.

Which understanding of Taqlīd?

The debate on *taqlīd* following a living legal scholar became a central one in Shi'i literature starting in the Safavid period; it acquired even greater importance with the emergence of the *marja'iyyat* in the Qajar period. Al-Shahīd al-Thānī wrote a treatise entitled *Risāla fī taqlīd al-mayyit* [The Treatise on the Imitation of Death], devoted entirely to this matter, and this issue was also at the heart of *Risāla al-ijtihād wa'l-akhbār*, by the well-known reviver of Usulism Muḥammad Bāqir "Waḥīd" al-Bihbahānī (m. 1206/1791-92 or 1208/1793-94). In the second part of his book, Abū al-Qāsim Khān essentially returns to his own conception of *taqlīd*. We can see two major differences between his undestanding and what the *uṣūlī*s propose.

On the one hand, because *ijtihād* is not legitimate, the believer must practice his *taqlīd* following the infallible Imam or a "trustworthy man."[128] In this second case, it is not a matter of a blind *taqlīd* as in the relation between a *muqallid* and a *mujtahid*, and whether or not this scholar is alive is not a determining factor: "Whether they are alive or dead, the word of the *mujtahid* is invalid (*mardūd*);"[129] "Relying on conjectures continues to be forbidden, and whether a *mujtahid* is dead or alive does not, therefore, change anything."[130] Every believer is also permitted to question this "trustworthy men" in the light of reason.[131] Of course, this *taqlīd* following the infallible Imams must also be practiced by the ulemas, who are "proofs" and "trustworthy men:" "But this *taqlīd* commanded by the Imams must not be carried out exclusively by ignorants, but also by the ulemas.

---

126 Stewart, *Islamic Legal Orthodoxy*, p. 195.
127 Ibid.
128 Abū al-Qāsim Khān Ibrāhīmī, *Ijtihād wa taqlīd*, pp. 186-187.
129 Ibid., p. 192.
130 Ibid., p. 216.
131 Ibid., p. 187.

The ulemas must practice their *taqlīd* following the Imām and use the *akhbārs* that is transmitted by a trustworthy man."[132] On the other hand, it is entirely possible to practice one's *taqlīd* following a dead person if that dead person is an infallible or a "trustworthy man:" "One can rely on the fatwa of a legal scholar that is based on the reading of an *akhbār*, whether the scholar is dead or alive."[133] We know, in fact, that the Shaykhī Kirmānīs, to this day, consult the treatise on legal practice by Muḥammad Karīm Khān, entitled *Jāma'*.[134] However, one must also know how to practice one's *taqlīd* following a living "trustworthy man," because it is among the duties of every believer to attempt to find such men.[135].

Therefore, it is obvious that one of the objectives of this work, which is essentially about the debate that energized the *uṣūlī* and *akhbārī* currents for centuries, is to present the *rukn-i rābi'* as the only doctrine that makes it possible to go beyond the doubts, the insufficiencies, and the errors of these two legal and theological methodologies.

132 Ibid., p. 247.

133 Ibid., p. 219.

134 Muḥammad Karīm Khān, *Jāma'* (translated from Arabic into Persian by Zayn al-'Ābidīn Ibrāhīmī and edited by Ḥasan Wakīl Zāda Ibrāhīmī), Qum, 1373sh./1994-95.

135 Abū al-Qāsim Khān Ibrāhīmī, *Ijtihād wa taqlīd*, p. 192.

Conclusions

Abū al-Qāsim Khān's *Ijtihād wa taqlīd* is a singular work. It is certainly the Shaykhī Kirmānī treatise that gives the greatest overview of the Shaykhī school's position on *ijtihād* as well as the intellectual history of Shi'ism, marked in particular by the longstanding antagonism between *uṣūlī* rationalism and *akhbārī* traditionalism. The Shaykhī positions on *fiqh* and its practices are also very clearly laid out in this work. Thus, it is definitely one of the most important intellectual refutations of Usulism written in the post-Safavid era. Neither al-Samāhijī, Shaykh Yūsuf Baḥrānī, Ḥusayn al-'Aṣfūr, Ni'matullāh al-Jazā'irī, nor Muḥammad Akhbārī Nayshābūrī seems to have written anything along these lines. In addition, *Ijtihād wa taqlīd* makes it possible to point out the central importance that Shaykhī literature has for the intellectual history of modern and contemporary Shi'ism. It would be particularly useful, in this context, to study the entirety of the body of legal work by the Shaykhī masters who came before Abū al-Qāsim Khān, in particular Shaykh Aḥmad al-Aḥsā'ī and Sayyid Kāẓim Rashtī.

While *Ijtihād wa taqlīd* can certainly be compared with the doctrinal statements of some *akhbārī* ulemas on this same question, its primary originality has to do with the centrality of the doctrine of the *rukn-i rābi'* in the argument as a whole, which, in a sense, bypasses the more literal reading of Akhbarism. In Kirmānī Shaykhism, believers are also called on to consult the *ḥadīth*s and to refer to them systematically, but the "genuine" scholar also plays an absolutely central role as the true interface between the Hidden Imām, the occult hierarchy, and the believers. These "trustworthy men," then, are in a position to write fatwas that carry authority for Shi'as. Thus, the search for answers to questions of *fiqh* can itself already becomes a spiritual journey. Confronted with the sadness that can invade the heart of every "true" Shi'a living in a world dominated by the forces of ignorance, in which it is therefore not surprising for *fiqh* to be distorted, faith in this occult hierarchy also comforts the believer.

On the other hand, the impact of the arguments of the Shaykhī masters and, in this case, of *Ijtihād wa taqlīd*, cannot be accurately understood without insisting on the profound organizational differences between these two currents of thought. The Shaykhī Kirmānī masters, unlike the *akhbārī* ulemas, thought of themselves as the representatives both of a school of thought and, at the same time, of a particularly cohesive community. And in fact, this communitarian organization is certainly what Akhbarism was cruelly lacking to ensure its survival in the early nineteenth century.

Nevertheless, in the same way as the *akhbārī* renewal of the seventeenth and eighteenth centuries may have pushed the *uṣūlī* clerics to overreact in order to safeguard their authority and their influence over Shi'i societies, one can ask whether the emergence of Shaykhism did not, paradoxically, further sharpen the process of hierarchization among the clergy, with the emergence of the *marja'iyyat* beginning in the second half of the nineteenth century.[1] While it is particularly difficult to evaluate the impact of works such as *Ijtihād wa taqlīd* on the intellectual and doctrinal history of Imamite Shi'ism starting in the second half of the twentieth century, it is not unthinkable that the publication of this book pushed some *uṣūlī* ulemas into assuming more radical stances.

1 On the paradoxical influence of Akhbarism on the evolution of *uṣūlī fiqh*, see Stewart, *Islamic Legal Orthodoxy*, p. 248.

BIBLIOTHECA ACADEMICA

Reihe Orientalistik – ISSN 1866-5071

Eine stets aktualisierte Liste der in dieser Reihe erscheinenden Titel finden Sie auf unserer Homepage http://www.ergon-verlag.de

Band 1
Kurz, Isolde
Vom Umgang mit dem anderen
Die Orientalismus-Debatte zwischen Alteritätsdiskurs und interkultureller Kommunikation
(vergriffen) 978-3-933563-88-0

Band 2
Abou-El-Ela, Nadia
ôwê nu des mordes, der dâ geschach ze bêder sît
Die Feindbildkonzeption in Wolframs 'Willehalm' und Usâmas 'Kitâb al-i'tibâr'
2001. 259 S. Kt.
€ 36,00 978-3-933563-93-4

Band 3
Bromber, Katrin
The Jurisdiction of the Sultan of Zanzibar and the Subjects of Foreign Nations
2001. 89 S. Kt.
€ 18,00 978-3-935556-65-1

Band 4
Fürtig, Henner (Hrsg.)
Islamische Welt und Globalisierung
Aneignung, Abgrenzung, Gegenentwürfe
(vergriffen) 978-3-935556-75-0

Band 5
Mutlu, Kays
Ismet Özel
Individualität und Selbstdarstellung eines türkischen Dichters
2004. 104 S. Kt.
€ 24,00 978-3-89913-328-8

Band 6
Jedlitschka, Anja
Weibliche Emanzipation in Orient und Okzident
Von der Unmöglichkeit, die Andere zu befreien
2004. 266 S. Kt.
€ 44,00 978-3-89913-339-4

Band 7
Bossaller, Anke
'Schlafende Schwangerschaft' in islamischen Gesellschaften
Entstehung und soziale Implikation einer weiblichen Fiktion
2004. 259 S. Kt.
€ 35,00 978-3-89913-363-9

Band 8
Möller, Reinhard (Hrsg.)
Islamismus und terroristische Gewalt
2004. 170 S. Kt.
€ 24,00 978-3-89913-365-3

Band 9
Arnold, Werner – Escher, Anton – Pfaffenbach, Carmella
Malula und Mᶜallōy
Erzählungen aus einem syrischen Dorf
2004. 248 S. zahlr. Farbabb. Fb.
€ 38,00 978-3-89913-369-1

Band 10
Schiffer, Sabine
Die Darstellung des Islam in der Presse
Sprache, Bilder, Suggestionen. Eine Auswahl von Techniken und Beispielen
(vergriffen) 978-3-89913-421-6

ERGON VERLAG · WÜRZBURG

Band 11
Wendt, Christina
Wiedervereinigung oder Teilung?
Warum das Zypern-Problem nicht gelöst wird
2006. 338 S. Kt.
€ 42,00 978-3-89913-495-7

Band 12
Görlach, Alexander
Der Heilige Stuhl im interreligiösen Dialog mit islamischen Akteuren in Ägypten und der Türkei
2007. 244 S. Kt.
€ 35,00 978-3-89913-558-9

Band 13
Pielow, Dorothee
Der Stachel des Bösen
Vorstellungen über den Bösen und das Böse im Islam
2008. 174 S. 4 Abb. Kt.
€ 25,00 978-3-89913-642-5

Band 14
Röhring, Christian
Orientalismus und Biografie
Religiöse Aspekte in Indienbildern deutschsprachiger Einwohner Indiens
2008. 376 S. 5 Tab. Kt.
€ 45,00 978-3-89913-646-3

Band 15
Ossenbach, Luise
Versmaß des Glaubens
Ein arabisches Gedicht zum Lob des Propheten von ʿAlam ad-Dīn as-Saḫāwī (st. 1245)
2009. 71 S. Kt.
€ 18,00 978-3-89913-721-7

Band 16
Ourghi, Mariella
Muslimische Positionen zur Berechtigung von Gewalt
Einzelstimmen, Revisionen, Kontroversen
2010. 190 S. Kt.
€ 32,00 978-3-89913-743-9

Band 17
Kowanda-Yassin, Ursula
Mensch und Naturverständnis im sunnitischen Islam
Ein Beitrag zum aktuellen Umweltdiskurs
2011. 208 S. Kt.
€ 28,00 978-3-89913-815-3

Band 18
Baumgarten, Jürgen
Die Ammarin
Beduinen in Jordanien zwischen Stamm und Staat
2011. 340 S. mehr. z.T. farb. Abb. Fb.
€ 48,00 978-3-89913-825-2

Band 19
Raih, Asmaa
Arabische Frauenliteratur und Interkulturalität
Eine Untersuchung ausgewählter Romane arabischer Autorinnen hinsichtlich der Konstitution der Fremdheit und der Beziehung zwischen Eigenem und Fremdem
2011. 192 S. mehr. S/w-Abb. Kt.
€ 28,00 978-3-89913-853-5

Band 20
Martinez-Weinberger, Elga
Romanschauplatz Saudi-Arabien
Transformationen, Konfrontationen, Lebensläufe
2011. XIV/235 S. Fb.
€ 38,00 978-3-89913-872-6

BIBLIOTHECA ACADEMICA

Reihe Orientalistik – ISSN 1866-5071

Band 21
Neufend, Maike
Das Moderne in der islamischen Tradition
Eine Studie zu Amīr ʿAbd al-Qādir al-Ǧazāʾirīs Verteidigung der islamischen Vernunft im 19. Jahrhundert
2012. 117 S. Kt.
€ 22,00 978-3-89913-891-7

Band 22
Wintermann, Jutta
Dichtung und Historie
Aspekte der Herrschaft Ḫosrous II. in Neẓāmīs *Ḫosrou-o Šīrīn*
2012. 108 S. 2 Kte. Kt.
€ 18,00 978-3-89913-890-0

Band 23
Sarkohi, Arash
Der Demokratie- und Menschenrechtsdiskurs der religiösen Reformer in Iran und die Universalität der Menschenrechte
2014. 239 S. Kt.
€ 32,00 978-3-95650-022-0

Band 24
Hermann, Denis
Kirmānī Shaykhism and the *ijtihād*
A Study of Abū al-Qāsim Khān Ibrāhīmī's *Ijtihād wa taqlīd*
2015. 50 S. Kt.
€ 12,00 978-3-95650-097-8

ERGON VERLAG · WÜRZBURG